FUN MAESTRO

A Solo Travel Revolution

BY YASEMIN AKTÜRK

Contents

PREFACE

From the moment we take our first steps, we begin a journey that is uniquely our own. Think back to those early milestones—learning to walk, then to speak, making your first friends. You walked into your first day of school alone, just like every other child. You learned how to read and write, forged new connections, and faced your first exams. And it didn't stop there. Every challenge you've faced, every test you've taken, every career milestone you've achieved—these moments were shaped by your own efforts. Still, you continue to master your own life alone. You've already proven that you can navigate life by yourself, so why not embrace the idea of traveling alone?

Yet, when it comes to traveling alone, many of us hesitate. We've been taught that experiences are only truly enjoyable when shared with others, that being alone is something to be ashamed of. Society often suggests that if we're alone, it's because we have no one to share our journey with. These ideas have conditioned us to do everything with others, leaving little time to understand what we truly want, who we are, and how to find joy when we're by ourselves. While sharing moments, emotions, and experiences with others is important and necessary—it's a fundamental part of being human—knowing ourselves and finding joy within ourselves is equally important. Perhaps even more so, but this is something we were never taught. That's why we now fear doing things alone, unable to cope with societal pressure or the boredom that comes with solitude. But the truth is, it's because we simply don't know how to spend time alone.

Solo travel is a powerful way to discover that. It's a chance to find out what truly makes you happy, what you like doing, and how to create joy from within. It's about learning to be your own best company, to celebrate your own victories, and to become the "Fun Maestro" of your own life—someone who can orchestrate joy and adventure, no matter the circumstances.

"Fun Maestro" is a term I created after becoming one myself, and that's why I wrote this book—to teach you how to become the Fun Maestro of your own life. It's not a strict, step-by-step guide on how to travel solo, but rather a collection of stories from my own travels, filled with the lessons I've learned along the way. My hope is that as you read, you'll find the encouragement you need to start your own solo adventures and the inspiration to become the Fun Maestro of your own life.

Are you ready?

CHAPTER
ONE

A JOURNEY OF SELF-DISCOVERY

I was sitting alone in a bar in Istanbul, enjoying my cocktail. The bar, located on a famous street in the Kadıköy neighborhood, was known for its open-minded atmosphere. By day, it was a café, but by night, it transformed into a lively boutique bar.

Housed in an old, three-story building, the entrance led directly to the second floor, with a bar to the right. Past the bar was a living room with vintage furniture, and at the far end, a DJ played house music under a red light. The living room opened up to a long rectangular garden, surrounded by high walls that separated it from neighboring buildings. The garden had benches along the walls, inviting everyone to sit together. In the center, people stood and danced, mingling in the open air.

The bar's unique layout made it easy for strangers to connect. As I enjoyed my drink, a woman with a warm smile approached and asked to sit with me. This was the charm of the place—a space that fostered spontaneous connections and new friendships.

I replied, "Yes, of course," to the woman. Little did I know that she would be the person to change my life with one sentence in the next couple of hours. She, too, was unaware.

"Are you alone here?" she asked.

"Yes, why does everyone keep asking me this? What's wrong with sitting alone and enjoying my own company?"

I found myself getting irritated each time that question popped up—whether I was sitting solo in a bar, dancing at a club, or even having a meal in a restaurant. As someone from Turkey, a country known for being social, it felt unusual to see people enjoying themselves alone. Don't get me wrong, I love to hang out with my friends too, but what if they have different interests? Should I put my hobbies on hold? Truth be told, I've been waiting for companionship for years. It's never been an issue for me to go somewhere and chill alone, whether grabbing coffee or having lunch. But doing those things by myself was a rarity. One day, feeling particularly down and in the mood to dance, I reached out to my friends, hoping they'd join me. No one showed up—for weeks, even months. That's when I made a decision: I'd go out on my own. How long could I keep waiting for someone to tag along? My list of activities to do kept growing. What was I waiting for? A boyfriend, a friend, more money? It was time to stop waiting and start living. That's how I ended up in that bar.

"No, there's nothing wrong with sitting alone. I came here solo, too. I'm Jülide, by the way, and my boyfriend is a DJ—he's playing now. I just want to enjoy his music. Plus, I admire people who can have a good time on their own," she replied.

I told her my name and we started chatting. I shared with her the reasons and moments when I began coming to this place by myself, realizing I didn't have a single friend with the same hobbies. While we mostly met in cafés or restaurants to talk about our lives, we didn't do much else together. When we did socialize, we opened up about our emotions, supported each other in our goals, and enjoyed each other's company. They were my friends, and I loved every moment with them. We talked, listened, and encouraged each other, but our hobbies didn't align.

My friends were more focused on creating marriages and families, while I was more interested in having fun, discovering, and seeking adventure. It was important for me to do something during the week after work, like going to the bar, but my friends preferred the weekends. I longed to do things like hiking, taking cooking classes, dancing, doing a sport, or traveling, but I often found myself alone in these pursuits because my interests were different from theirs.

"Yasemin, just follow your own path and pursue your own hobbies. You'll meet people like you along the way," she said.

Jülide ignited a spark in my mind. I kept repeating that sentence for days. She was right. Why hadn't I thought of it before? Following my own hobbies, my own path, and meeting people who share the same interests sounded much simpler than trying to convince my friends to join me in an activity.

A few days after our conversation, I began thinking about moving forward and making plans to travel. I had always dreamed of visiting Rome since my childhood. There was something special about it, and even though I had only seen it on the Internet, I felt a unique connection with Rome. This connection stemmed from my deep interest in Greek and Roman architecture. I even took courses at university about reading sculptures and understanding their historical periods, despite studying computer engineering. I made up my mind not to wait for anyone to join me, so I bought a ticket to Rome, deciding to follow my own path and meet people along the way, just like Jülide advised me. That became my life motto: Follow your own path. Follow your heart.

At that time, my budget wasn't exactly stable, but I made the decision to go for it anyway and find a more affordable way. I was part of a Facebook group where people shared their travel stories. Through that, I discovered hostel options, which were much cheaper compared to hotels. I began checking out hostels in Rome and found one exclusively for women. Excited, I made a booking and extended it to Florence. As I started to prepare for my first solo trip, I couldn't contain my excitement and shared my plans with everyone around me.

My friends were surprised when I mentioned staying in a hostel. It was new to them, and they bombarded me with questions:

Why would you share a room with others?

What if something happens while you sleep, like an assault?

What if someone steals something from you?

Why is it only for women? What if it is a brothel?

How will you manage to travel alone?

Who will take your pictures?

Won't you get bored being alone all the time?

Why don't you consider going on a tour?

After talking with them, I felt nervous. I had never considered that staying in a women-only hostel might be an issue. Their concerns about it being a disreputable place or the fear of someone trying to harm me were never on my mind before, and suddenly, they became worries that I couldn't shake off.

But what about my path? I yearned to meet people who shared my interests and to follow my own dreams. How long could I wait for someone to join me? How long could I wait to have more money? No, that night when I spoke with Jülide, I had made a decision, and I wouldn't alter my plans. I stopped sharing my travel plans with those who questioned me and continued reading powerful stories on the Facebook group where women shared their travel experiences.

Within the same group, someone mentioned a website called Couchsurfing, which facilitates connections between travelers and locals. Intrigued by the concept, I created an account and shared my travel dates. Surprisingly, many locals reached out, some even offering a place to stay. However, the idea of staying in a stranger's home seemed too risky for me, and I wasn't comfortable placing that level of trust in someone I had never met. Instead, I opted to meet some of them outside for a drink.

Four months had passed since I bought tickets for Rome, and everything was ready for my solo trip. The day had come to fly out from Istanbul. Despite feeling a bit nervous, I was filled with happiness and determination. I had no doubt in my mind. The main emotion was the excitement of exploring Rome and, along the way, learning more about myself.

Arriving in Rome, I went through passport control, then began searching for a bus to reach the women-only hostel. When I approached a few people for help, I faced a language barrier as they couldn't speak English. However, their helpful gestures and body language spoke louder than words. It's true what they say—body language works everywhere, always. Eventually, I successfully reached the hostel.

After checking in, I headed to the room where I would be staying for the next couple of days. In it were three other women. One of them, a beautiful artist from Australia, had a radiant smile. I learned that she came to Rome to participate in an art exhibition. Shortly after, I met another woman who was from Chile. She was incredibly friendly, and we engaged in a pleasant conversation.

I was overflowing with excitement and happiness. The entire day had been a unique challenge, but the best challenge of my life. I wasn't sure if I could find the bus, locate the hostel, or communicate in English. Questions about what a hostel was, what the people there would be like, why it was just for women, and if it was safe, buzzed in my mind. However, I had overcome those uncertainties, and I was already in a hostel where everyone was incredibly nice. Meeting all those people had been the highlight of my experience so far. Filled with energy, I was ready to explore the city, meet new people, sip coffee, indulge in tiramisu, marvel at the Colosseum, and more.

With just my phone, a power bank, and a bit of money, I left the hostel in Trastevere. As a budget traveler, I preferred walking over spending money on bus tickets. Campo de' Fiori was the first landmark I visited, then I explored several other places: Piazza Navona, the Pantheon, and Piazza Venezia. During my wanderings, I met an Italian guy named Manuelle through Couchsurfing. We visited the Spanish Steps, had a delightful conversation, and then I walked back to the hostel. It started to rain on the way, but I kept walking, feeling like I was in a movie amidst the historical buildings.

It hadn't even been a full day in Rome, yet it felt like two to three days had passed because of all the things I had done. I was genuinely happy, happier than I had ever been. Thoughts about home, work, my identity, the need for friends, who would take my picture, hostel safety, and various concerns, were nowhere in my mind. I was fully immersed in the moment, relishing the joy of living my dream.

On another day when I woke up, the Chilean woman had already departed the hostel, but she left a sweet note and a chocolate for me. Remember what my friends warned me about staying in hostels? Yet, here was my experience—warm and thoughtful gestures.

Throughout the day, I explored many places, and in the morning, a guy I had met through Couchsurfing who was also traveling in Rome, Nika, joined me. We started with a coffee together and then walked to the Trevi Fountain, taking millions of pictures along the way, with Nika acting as my photographer. Then we went to Piazza del Popolo and Villa Borghese, spending some time there before heading back to the old city and visiting the Pantheon together. It was my second visit, but this time I went inside. On the first day, I had just walked around the Pantheon. Finally, we parted ways somewhere close to the Colosseum.

It was so much fun to explore the city with another traveler. I was meeting people who shared my interests on my journey, just like Jülide had said. It's amazing how powerful words can be. They have the potential to either break our spirits or create a whole new life. We should be mindful of the words we allow into our subconscious minds.

In the evening, I met the "Roman Statue," an Italian guy from Couchsurfing who made me feel like I was in a fairy tale. Many people had written to me from Couchsurfing, but I especially wanted to hang out with the Roman Statue because his profile was filled with pictures from around the world. I wanted to meet an adventurous person and learn about traveling. However, I was pleasantly surprised because, in real life, he was nothing like his profile picture. He had a cool, striking presence, with a physique that resembled that of a Roman statue, and a distinctly Italian face, complete with a prominent nose like those in classical sculptures. There was something undeniably handsome about him, and I was instantly drawn to him.

The Roman Statue took me on a walking tour around the Roman Forum. We passed through some narrow streets and saw some small fountains. He shared a beautiful love story about one of the fountains, saying that if a couple drinks from it together, they will fall in love forever. Then we walked to a secluded spot with an elevated view of the Roman Forum, where we could see a slideshow projected on a historical building. To add to the enchantment, he pulled out a pizza and a bottle of wine from his backpack. I was surprised and it felt incredibly romantic because he had thought of all the details. Even though we had just met, it was like a date—nice conversation, delicious food, and a beautiful setting. The Roman Statue became even more handsome to me at that moment. After finishing our pizza, we went to a local bar in Trastevere where his friend was playing the guitar. I mingled with many Italians at the bar, dancing with each of them and, of course, with the Roman Statue.

We stayed at the bar for a long time, but I lost track of time, as I was so engrossed in the moment. We were drunk and walked along the river, holding hands, laughing, and kissing. At one point, I looked up at the sky and felt incredibly fortunate, thinking that this was a special gift for being brave enough to travel alone and taking all those steps.

The Roman Statue asked if I was hungry, and I realized I was. His car was parked nearby, so we walked a long way to get to it. In his car, he played Italian music from the radio, and I felt like I was truly experiencing the city with an Italian. He took me to a döner place run by Turkish people, which was interesting for me to see in Italy. We enjoyed our meal together, and the next day, we parted ways. Before leaving Rome, I met with him again. We still stay in touch occasionally, with him liking some of my pictures on social media, but we haven't met again. It remains one of the nicest and most romantic memories for me that I will never forget.

Before that trip, I often worried about being alone and getting bored, wondering who would take my pictures and whether I would enjoy the experience without company. However, the reality was so different. My concerns were unnecessary because I met so many people, both locals and fellow travelers, who turned my journey into an incredible adventure. I wasn't just touring; I was genuinely exploring and connecting with the places I visited. I danced with locals in neighborhood bars, strolled through the city with them, listened to their music, and heard their stories. I went from worrying about taking pictures to fully immersing myself in the culture and having unforgettable experiences.

In total, I spent 10 days visiting Rome, Florence, and Prague for just 2 days. Prague wasn't initially on my list, but a month before my trip, I had interviews with a global company for a job position. They invited me for a final interview in Prague, so it became a part of my travel plan.

During those 10 days, I met incredible people from around the world. Some were younger, some older, some students, and some working. Some were traveling with friends, but most were solo travelers. A few were even traveling the world. Spending time with them led to engaging, open-minded conversations.

When I initially bought a ticket for Rome, my goal was simply to explore a city I had always wanted to see, follow my own path, and meet like-minded people. However, while reading stories on Facebook before going to Rome, I came across many inspiring tales of global travel. And finally meeting those world travelers during my trip motivated me to become one of them and explore the world. Why not? Those 10 days were the best of my life. I connected with people from all corners of the globe, most of whom shared similar hobbies. I experienced immense joy, encountered no threats, and realized that solo travel was not as challenging as initially anticipated. Fueled by the memories of those 10 days, a new ambition took root within me. I resolved that my next goal would be nothing short of traveling around the world.

It was October 2016. With strong determination, I made a plan: in three months, paying off all my credit card debt, and in another six months, saving money. My big plan was quitting my job and starting a journey around the world. I didn't want to delay this dream for another year, as waiting for the elusive "enough money" would always keep it out of reach.

As January started, I spent my days saving money and researching travel ideas. I started planning to kick off my global adventure in Rome, as it held a special place in my heart. To get ready, I bought a one-way ticket for July 15, 2017, starting from Istanbul, my home.

To save money, I made several changes to my lifestyle. I began eating at home and only met with friends for a drink, mostly coffee, which was cheaper than dining out together. I almost stopped going to bars and clubs, which also reduced my spending on taxis as I relied more on public transportation. I started working out at home instead of paying for a gym membership. I used to go to fancy skincare beauty centers, but I stopped those visits. I also stopped buying clothes and other non-essential items. The only things I purchased for my big trip were a backpack, a pair of nice everyday shoes, and flip-flops. Additionally, I was staying with my family, which allowed me to save most of my money.

While getting ready, I realized I needed a visa for my journey in Europe, so I successfully got one, allowing me to explore the continent for a month. I had a clear plan in my mind: start in Rome, travel across Europe for a month, and then head to South America and Africa. Afterward, find a way to earn money while traveling and continue the adventure in Asia and the rest of the world. However, there were no more details; everything would be decided in the moment. I just wanted to go with the flow.

You might be wondering why I opted for South America and Africa as my destinations. It all boils down to dance. Dancing has been an integral part of my life for as long as I can remember. I've been dancing since childhood. My mom always said that I started walking at a very early age and was dancing from that moment on. Although I never took a formal dance class, I have a natural talent for capturing movements and learning any dance just by watching. Whether I'm bored, happy, or sad, dancing is my go-to expression—it's like second nature. I can lose myself in dance for hours, forgetting about everything else. My love for dancing extends beyond just the physical activity; it's a passion I want to share with people who feel the same way. I believed I would find those like-minded individuals on my journey through South America and Africa, because I adore their music, the way they dance, and the joy they find in the rhythm.

Choosing South America and Africa was not solely about dance; it was also driven by my fascination with the rich cultures these continents hold. Each place has its own unique charm, and I was drawn to explore the diverse cultures and stunning landscapes they offer. While I'd love to visit other continents too, my financial situation limited my choices, and the rest depended on job options that I would find along the way.

In July 2017, I bid farewell to my job as a senior software engineer at a large company in Turkey. With seven years of experience under my belt, I embarked on a new adventure. On the 15th of July, I found myself in Rome, marking the commencement of my global travel journey. During my one-month trip across Europe, I explored Rome, Naples, Paris, Amsterdam, Barcelona, Valencia, and Madrid. I decided to visit them while I was there, without anything set in stone on the plan. Throughout this adventure, I encountered many incredible individuals.

While there were occasional minor hiccups with some of the people I stayed with via Couchsurfing, the overall experience was exceptionally positive. For instance, at the beginning of my big journey, I was in Rome, staying at a hostel. I had planned to head to Naples the next day, but then I received a message on Couchsurfing inviting me to a hip-hop concert in Rome. After chatting with the person who invited me, I decided to extend my stay in Rome and join him and his friends for the concert. However, since the hostel was fully booked, I ended up staying at their place after the concert until the following day. Despite having discussed sleeping arrangements beforehand, he unexpectedly suggested we share a bed, although there were extra ones available. I declined and chose to sleep in a different bed, but felt uneasy and couldn't sleep, worried about my safety. At 5 a.m., I quietly left the apartment. A similar situation occurred in Spain, which led me to stop using Couchsurfing for accommodation suggestions. Despite selecting hosts with many positive reviews and taking precautions like chatting for several days and meeting in public places first, I realized that some people used the platform to have casual sex, which was not my goal.

In spite of the challenges I faced with two Couchsurfing hosts, I still met many wonderful people through the platform who shared similar interests and became lasting friends. Additionally, I connected with other travelers along the way, forming bonds that made my journey even more memorable. During all my trips, I shared delightful local meals with fellow travelers and danced with them in clubs. In Naples, I explored the ruins of Pompeii with a group of history enthusiasts. In Amsterdam, I enjoyed a free river tour and stayed in the house of a friend of other travelers I met in Paris. In Barcelona, I danced the night away at a beach party and went to Valencia with another traveler where we explored the city. In Naples, a local gave me a walking city tour about history, followed by a motorcycle tour to the higher parts of the city, and then cooked a traditional Italian meal for me.

Whether spending a few hours or a few days together, the fun we had left lasting impressions. I've gone on to meet some of these newfound friends in different countries, years later, and our conversations are as lively as ever. These fellow travelers have become my best friends. Typically, we make plans to reunite somewhere in the world for a short time, exploring together before everyone resumes their individual journeys. Bonding with these free-spirited souls has enriched my travels, all while allowing me to remain on my own unique path.

After a month exploring Europe, my next stop was Peru. There, I fulfilled a dream that was at the top of my bucket list after Rome—visiting Machu Picchu. Machu Picchu felt like a spiritual place with a unique energy and vibration. The natural beauty was extraordinary, and thinking about how the ancient people created a city atop mountains with such interesting and unique knowledge made the place even more remarkable. The natural setting, the view, everything, was so fascinating and left me in awe. Standing amidst the ancient city and realizing my dreams was truly incredible.

Following Peru, I ventured into Bolivia, which presented its own set of challenges, especially since English wasn't as widely understood, and body language wasn't as effective. To overcome this hurdle, I made the decision to take a short Spanish course. I headed to Sucre, where I dedicated two weeks to learning the basics of Spanish. This newfound language skill significantly eased my travels and opened up a whole new level of exploration.

In Chile, I experienced the warmth of Chilean hospitality, which made me feel at home in a foreign land. As I traveled through Argentina, I discovered how much the simplicity of travel and living close to nature could transform me in a positive way. I found immense happiness in the natural beauty around me, and it was there that I began to embrace a more adventurous side of myself.

In Brazil, I immersed myself in the vibrant culture, experiencing the fun and camaraderie of Brazilian friendship and the infectious rhythms of their music. My journey through Colombia pushed my adventurous spirit even further, as I became more daring and willing to take on new challenges.

In Mexico, I learned the art of traveling on a small budget, realizing how little I needed to find joy and fulfillment on the road. Finally, in Cuba, I lived my dream through the enchanting music and captivating dances that filled the air. It was in those moments that I truly felt like I was living the life I had always dreamed of.

The adventure was enriching and the desire to keep going was strong. However, reality caught up with me as my bank account hit zero. With no savings or job waiting for me in Istanbul, my dream came to an end, exhausted down to my last cent.

How long I cried, I do not know. This time, saying goodbye was exceptionally challenging. Perhaps the most difficult farewell I've ever experienced in my life...

Eight months ago, I left my home to explore and search for a city that resonates with my soul. Eventually, I discovered it. Or maybe, it discovered me.

It's reminiscent of my childhood. Streets may be dirty, but they're brimming with children. Buildings may be old, but the sense of neighborhood is profound. Despite poverty, there's an abundance of humanity.

It goes beyond my childhood too. The city is alive with music and dance, a vibrancy I've never encountered in other countries but always dreamed of.

People stroll with speakers, dancing on the streets at their whim, much like how I want to live.

Music echoes at all hours from various sources: cars, houses, streets, schools...

If someone starts singing, another is always ready to join in or dance. No one complains about the volume, even if the music plays past midnight.

It's the only place where everyone shares the same musical interests as me and revels in the kind of fun I love. They cherish music and dance just as much as I do.

Perhaps not mojito, but piña colada has become my favorite cocktail. Thanks to it, a beautiful tale unfolded with the best music, dance, and delightful people.

I didn't realize how swiftly time flew, and I had to bid farewell to my entire piña colada story.

It's like a dream I've been yearning for during these eight months, abruptly interrupted by someone waking me at the peak of its beauty. I long to return to that dream, but continuing from where it left off seems impossible...

I miss Havana and my piña colada story.

Those words spilled out onto paper as I flew back to Turkey from Havana. Sadly, I'd already spent all my money and had to return to Turkey. Tears streamed down my face during the flight, and I continued to cry until no tears remained.

I had just discovered so much about myself, found happiness in the moment, and felt like the most beautiful woman in the world. Yes, the most beautiful woman in the world. Because when you travel alone, it's not just about going to new places; it's like going deep inside yourself. With each step, you start feeling better about who you are, and that inner transformation makes you shine with a beauty that goes beyond just looks. Everybody, including yourself, sees that beauty and embraces it. And I cried, not wanting to lose that feeling again.

It wasn't just about the feeling; it was also about losing a dream— the dream of a place where everyone danced on the streets as if in a musical. I had been searching for it throughout my journey. I thought it would be Brazil, but it wasn't. Then I thought maybe Colombia, but it wasn't. Maybe I was too optimistic to envision such a country. But when I landed in Cuba, I saw that it was real. People on the streets were walking with huge speakers, and everybody was dancing all the time, anywhere. All were like professional dancers, and there was always someone to grab my hand and dance with me. I was the main character of the musical, living my dream. I had finally accessed the nirvana of happiness, but the dream ended with my last cent. Like all beautiful things, it had to end. I was sad, not just because my journey was over, but because, at the same time, I had lost my dream.

It was 4 a.m., and I stood in the doorway of my house. When my father opened the door, he was surprised to see me so soon. Even though my family knew I'd be back, they didn't expect me this early. My mom, dad, and siblings all woke up to welcome me, thrilled to see me after eight months. However, I wasn't as happy as them. After enjoying the adventures of traveling alone and backpacking for a long time, it was tough to accept that it had ended.

As a fellow traveler once wisely said, when you travel for an extended period, it becomes like a poison in your blood, and the desire to do it again and again lingers. True enough, that sentiment resonated with me.

Before starting the journey, when I quit my job, I thought I would never have the same job when I came back because if you take a long break, nobody wants to hire you again—they think you've forgotten all your coding skills. I had accepted that risk, and it was totally worth it.

During my travels, I learned that I am capable of anything. I climbed big rocks without any equipment, found my way even when lost, and communicated effectively despite language barriers. There were no limits—only the ones I imposed on myself. With these newfound feelings of high self-esteem, courage, and self-worth, I returned home knowing that I deserved a better salary than before and that I could continue my career from where I left off. It didn't matter what others said—I would set the rules.

I requested a salary that was three times more than my previous one. I studied and learned new things while applying for jobs and covered many gaps in my knowledge in a short time. My mind was relaxed, focused on the goal, and confident in my abilities. I passed many interviews and faced rejections as well. Some employers found my salary expectations unrealistic, but others offered something close. I never changed my attitude or lowered my standards, regardless of the interview outcomes. Eventually, I secured a better job as a senior software engineer with a salary three times more than my previous job. The journey made me realize that I deserved more than what was given to me, and I would only accept what I deserved—and it happened.

Self-worth was not just about salary; it was about many things, including my appearance. Before starting that journey, I felt fat because my colleagues told me I needed to lose weight, even though I wore small sizes. Growing up in Turkey, it felt like I had to be extra small to be considered fit. However, during my journey, many people complimented my body, and I started to feel better about it. Then I realized how perfect my body is. Who would refer to someone as "fat" when they have visible abdominal muscles? I realized I do not have to fit others' standards; I have my own standards. I am the standard.

What happened next was magical: When I came back, even though I had gained a few pounds, everybody started to compliment me. They told me how my body was super sexy and how fit I looked. Actually, nothing changed about my body, except my mindset.

The change in mindset happened because of the journey. The journey went deep within me. I discovered myself so deeply and loved the version that I had at the end. That brought so much confidence to my life, and it was the thing shining within me, and everybody was attracted to it.

Solo travel is a life-changing experience and a perfect way to explore yourself. Everyone should try it at least once. I know that it is not an easy decision and requires some courage, but I am here to guide you and provide the encouragement you need.

CHAPTER

TWO

MANIFESTING THE COURAGE AND FINDING ENCOURAGEMENT

The journey toward encouragement begins with action and you have already started to take action by purchasing this book. I know the idea of traveling solo might feel like a major leap, but if you start making small changes in your everyday life, these little adjustments could eventually lead you to embark on your first solo trip. Just remember, the small steps are what matter most.

Before deciding to venture out on a solo journey to Rome, I had already taken several significant steps. It was not a one-day decision, even though it may seem that way. Honestly, going to a café or restaurant alone had never been an issue for me, but the thought of going to a bar or club solo was something I had never considered, much like traveling alone. However, circumstances led me to break that barrier. No one around my age (29) shared an interest in the activities I craved. One day, I decided to step out of my comfort zone and visited the bar known for its sociable atmosphere. The bar changed many things in my life. But I was doing many things, not just visiting a bar; I was socializing with random people in different ways and trying new hobbies alone. I joined online meetups, attended cooking and painting classes, participated in running groups, visited museums, went for nature hikes, attended concerts and theater shows alone, and took group guitar courses. Everything I did increased my self-esteem, showing that I could have fun without needing anyone else. So, you need to prove to yourself that you can do it, then you will have the encouragement.

Taking the first step is crucial. You don't have to decide to embark on solo travel in one day. Make it a gradual part of your life and witness the progress. Start by purchasing a ticket for a city you want to explore a few months later. Buying the ticket is important because it forces you to step out of your comfort zone. The trip does not have to be long; keep it short—choose a city in another country or your own. This serves as your initiation into solo travel, just as I did. When I talked with Jülide, the woman in the bar, and decided to go to Rome, I bought my ticket. I did all the other research later. If I hadn't bought the ticket, I might have kept waiting for the next opportunity, which may never have come. Who knows?

Leading up to the trip, take small steps like going to a café alone, dining solo, hiking alone, or visiting a bar by yourself. Engage in activities you enjoy, spending at least one hour each week in your own company. Discover what you need and relish during your alone time. This journey isn't solely about learning to travel alone; it's about spending meaningful time with yourself.

Every person should enjoy their own company. Spending time with ourselves increases independence and self-esteem, reducing dependency on others. Take those first steps to boost your self-esteem. If going to a café alone is easy for you, try something different—something you've always wanted to try but never did, something you were waiting for someone else to do with you.

As you become more comfortable going solo, add another layer to your life by engaging in activities with people you don't know. Join classes and clubs for cooking, hiking, books, or running. These experiences will enhance your communication skills, making it easier to be social with anyone. However, be sure that you join the group activities after engaging in solo time. When we can enjoy our own company, we are better equipped to appreciate being with any group. If we don't find joy in our solo experiences, we might focus more on interactions in the group setting than on our own enjoyment. That can make the process tiring, and you will likely get bored at some point.

If you're unsure about which activity to pursue, explore the options you already have and search for new ones. The ultimate goal is self-discovery—understanding what you enjoy doing alone, revealing your hobbies, and recognizing your capabilities. Take the time to figure out what you like and what you don't. Trust me, you'll unearth many aspects of yourself that you might not have been aware of before.

Before my first trip, I experimented with various activities in search of something enjoyable. That's when I joined a running club. Meeting three to four times a week, people from different age groups gathered to run together at different locations across the beautiful city of Istanbul. And it was free, organized by a famous shoe brand. The routes were carefully chosen, showcasing the city's scenery. Participants were organized into groups based on their running level, each group running at different times. Through this club, I formed connections with many individuals, and running gradually became a significant part of my routine. Despite working until 6 p.m. every day, I eagerly joined these running sessions, which often took me at least two hours to return home. The joy I derived from this went beyond just socializing; I genuinely relished every moment of it. Making friends was an added bonus. As my connections deepened, I began participating in gym activities with them and eventually entered a marathon in Istanbul. Unfortunately, right before the marathon, I sustained an injury, prompting me to slow down and opt for less strenuous exercise. This marked the beginning of my journey into regular workouts. Before, I didn't think I liked exercising because I thought it meant using machines at the gym. But then, in the running club, I discovered HIIT (High-Intensity Interval Training), and it made me really enjoy working out. HIIT includes things like push-ups and burpees, where I don't have time to think too much—I just focus on the exercise. Doing these intense workouts helps me concentrate on the moment and clear my mind. I found the kind of exercise I like while discovering myself, and it still works well for me six years later. Because it's related to sports, it has given me a big boost in confidence. It changed the way I see myself and the world. I began to realize how strong I am and how good I am at sports. It automatically affected the way I communicate with others too. It's all connected—engaging in an activity not only boosts self-esteem but also, in the case of sports, enhances body confidence. When shared with others, it increases opportunities for communication, further boosting self-esteem. This positive cycle leads to a greater appreciation of one's own company, making you someone others want to spend time with. Trust me, through this process, you'll become a human magnet that everyone wants to spend time with and you will find the encouragement to do anything alone.

One of my colleagues, intrigued by my solo travels, began spending more time with me after my first solo trip. She asked questions and tried to emulate my experiences, wanting to feel the same way I did. However, she found it challenging to do things I did so effortlessly due to her own biases. She raised concerns like, "Don't you worry about what others think when you eat alone?" or "Aren't you bored going to a bar by yourself?" and "Do you not feel embarrassed approaching strangers?"

It's normal to have such biases; I had my own biases as well. However, we only live our lives once, and prioritizing what others think over our own desires is unfair to ourselves—almost like committing a crime against our own authenticity. If we don't stand up for ourselves, no one else will. When we are confident in ourselves, others won't find the courage to judge us; instead, they may seek to emulate our self-assuredness.

People often tend to criticize what they cannot do themselves. Forget about what others might think, take that first step for yourself, and believe me, people won't judge someone who feels good about eating alone or making friends easily.

So, my ex-colleague began taking small steps to overcome her biases. First, she decided to have a solo lunch at work, which felt like a big deal for her. Then, she ventured into cafés alone. Of course, we did some activities together or with friends because doing everything solo could be boring. However, she made sure to engage in solo pastimes to enjoy her own company. As she gained more confidence, she took solo trips within her own country, and eventually to a different one. Throughout her journey, she faced moments of boredom and happiness, learning valuable lessons for the next time. She discovered her limits, hobbies, and, most importantly, herself. Then, she ventured into trying hostels, something she had never done before. Despite not being a fluent English speaker, she tackled the language barrier by taking an English course, making socializing easier. It took her three years to feel prepared for a more extended trip. During those years, she connected with other Turkish travelers worldwide, joining some of them on trips. Her adventures began in Asia and expanded to Africa. Now, she's a well-known influencer, still exploring and sharing her experiences.

It's incredible to think that she started as someone hesitant even to have a solo lunch at work. How did she do it? She began with small steps. So, if you're thinking about embarking on your own journey, start with small steps too, just as I mentioned earlier. Keep in mind that everybody's steps are different, so each of us will discover a unique path. However, the result will be perfect for anyone willing to take those steps.

Taking small steps is not limited to discovering new hobbies or activities; it also involves extending our abilities. One such ability is being open to having conversations with anyone. This openness creates more opportunities to meet new people wherever you are. If you keep telling yourself, "I can't talk to strangers," you might limit yourself. However, if you say, "I can talk when there's an opportunity," you create the chance to engage in conversations. It's a small mindset shift, but the results are significant. Trust me, I've experienced all these aspects in my life.

I was in Colombia, and a girl, Nara, joined me in traveling to another city. While we were waiting for a bus to Santa Marta from Costeño Beach, two guys came over and started waiting too. I could tell they were travelers, so I turned to ask them directly:

"Where are you going?"

"Palomino. You?" the first guy said.

"Santa Marta. What will you do in Palomino? I have never heard of it."

"We will go tubing. It is very famous there."

"What is it?"

"You just jump inside of a car tire and go on a river. What will you do in Santa Marta?" the second guy asked.

"We haven't planned yet. How long does it take to go to Palomino?"

"Two hours? Why don't you join us?"

"Where will you stay? Can my friend Nara and I find a place too?"

"I am sure you can find space in any hostel. There are many."

Then I asked Nara, and we both decided to join the friends we would dub the "Tubing Duo." Even though I did not understand exactly what was involved, I wanted to go tubing because they were so excited. I did not want to miss it, whatever it was. Besides, it was only two hours away from our current location, and we could continue to Santa Marta afterward.

We went to the hostel together and found space for two days. When we booked tubing for the next day, that's when I learned all the details. The next day, everyone gathered at the hostel reception in their swimsuits. They advised us not to take phones or anything important as we would be jumping into the river.

I can swim, but I've never felt comfortable in deep water. So, I asked how deep it was, and one of the guys in charge told me not much, maximum 150 centimeters. I thought, "Okay, not a problem. Shorter than my height."

They gave each person a tire, and some motorcycle drivers took us towards our destination. The drivers dropped us off in the jungle and told us to jump into the river from that point. They explained that we would be on the river for about two hours, and it would eventually join the ocean. When it did, we needed to jump and head to the beach; otherwise, we'd end up in the ocean.

As everyone jumped into the river with their tires, I encountered a challenge. The river was moving, and so were we on top of it. There was a small curve, and suddenly my tire got stuck. Everyone was drifting in the current, and nobody could help or wait for me. They were getting further away, yelling, "Yasemin, try to catch us." I was alone, trying to save the tire. I wanted to jump into the water and move the tire with my hand, but it seemed too deep, and you know how uncomfortable I am in deep water. Maybe half an hour passed, and another tubing group arrived. One of the guys noticed me:

"What are you doing there?" he asked.

"Trying to save myself."

"Are you alone?"

"No, my group has already left."

"Oh, did they leave you? We won't leave you. Try to move the tire a bit into the flow."

While I was trying to follow his instructions, his friends gathered on the water inside their tires. They created a huge tire combination by putting one leg into another person's tire, making themselves slower to catch up with me on the river. Eventually, I joined the flow, and along the way, they caught my hand. One of them put his leg onto my tire, and I connected one of my legs to his tire. Now, we were all drifting on the river together.

They were international travelers just like me, from different parts of the world—four men and three women. Some of them knew each other beforehand, while others had met while traveling. They had rented a van and decided to tour Colombia, with plans to head to Panama next. They even invited me to join them.

They were the funniest people I had ever met, constantly joking with each other, laughing about their shared stories, and truly enjoying the moment. They made me laugh about the situation I was in, being stuck in the river, and turned it into a fun experience for all of us. They were so well prepared too. I had left everything at the hostel and just brought myself, but they had everything they needed inside a waterproof bag: sunscreen, beer, chips, and even speakers for music. We were partying on the river.

At some point, we spotted the ocean, a signal to jump into the water and head to the beach. There, I saw Nara and the Tubing Duo. They had been waiting for me, as I was an hour late. I exchanged phone numbers with the people from the river and later met them for breakfast.

Looking back on this experience, if I hadn't struck up a conversation with the Tubing Duo while waiting for the bus, I would have missed out on this incredible story. The lesson: be open to talking with others. You might assume I'm the only one in this story open to conversation, but that's not the case. Also, you might think that I am a conversation starter, and yes, I am, but not always. The guys I chatted with while waiting for the bus were open to talking. Although they did not start the conversation, they continued it, explained their plans, and even invited me. As for the guys I met on the river, they started the conversation and I was open to talking. They engaged in conversation while drifting on the river and went out of their way to catch up with me. Therefore, you don't always need to initiate a conversation, but remain receptive and willing to engage when approached by others. This is particularly important when traveling solo. Even if you don't take the lead, there will always be someone, and being receptive can lead to new adventures in your life, increasing opportunities to socialize.

I have shared various steps to find encouragement for travel. Don't forget to start by purchasing a flight ticket for a few months later and then take small steps to boost your self-esteem. Discover ways to enjoy your own company and actively engage with others by joining group activities that you like. Most importantly, be open to conversation.

The steps may be challenging, especially for those who have never attempted them before. However, as you begin to take action, you'll learn that they become easier, and you'll find encouragement from within.

Remember, everyone has their unique capabilities and boundaries. If you find it challenging to converse with foreigners or take an extra step, it doesn't mean solo travel is off the table. The aim is to boost self-esteem and seize opportunities during our travels. People vary; you might discover your own way to travel solo and relish the experience. When you find joy within yourself, you will have fun anywhere, and that self-assurance will empower you to explore the world.

THREE

THE POWER IN IGNORING NEGATIVE IDEAS

I am sure there will be people who might try to persuade you against solo travel or anything they find challenging. It happens, always. Don't let their fears or bad experiences become your own. If you do, you won't get to where you want to be, and you might miss finding your own way. These people could be your family, friends, colleagues, or someone you meet while traveling. Don't adopt their fears. Remember, this is the golden rule, even more crucial than what we talked about in the previous chapter.

I encountered numerous individuals who attempted to instill their fears in me, and some of them succeeded. When I was planning my first solo trip to Rome, I eagerly shared my excitement with everyone around me. However, instead of encouragement, they filled my mind with fears. I started worrying about potential dangers, like the risk of assault in the women-only hostel they described as "weird." Some even planted the idea that I'd get bored and struggle to find things to do alone. Carrying these fears and worries with me, I arrived in Rome feeling like I was taking a massive risk, almost a life-or-death situation in my mind. It wasn't easy, but I was determined to face whatever came my way. Meeting nice people there helped me get rid of those fears bit by bit. Then I decided not to let what others think control my journey and relished my travel with freedom. If I had listened to them, I wouldn't have dared to plan my extensive trip around the world.

Avoiding negative thoughts isn't only about the people you know. There might be occasions when you come across locals who unintentionally make their own country seem frightening. Don't take them too seriously. Stay careful about what you do, but that doesn't mean you have to change your plans or feel scared.

While chatting with two Italians from Rome in a restaurant, I mentioned my plan to travel to Naples next. Their advice was, "If you can travel without any issues in Naples, you can travel anywhere in the world. Naples is not safe, so be extremely careful." I felt really scared because they were from Italy, and I thought they must know better.

When I arrived, I found it challenging to venture outside. I felt like someone might be following me, and was constantly anticipating that something bad would happen. It significantly affected my experience, making the first day quite terrible, and I couldn't enjoy anything. I wanted to leave but I had already paid for my reservations. Then, I connected with Luigi through Couchsurfing who happened to be from Naples. He reassured me that there was no need to feel in danger in Naples. He showed me around, took me to many historical places, and introduced me to some local people. The next day, my perception of Naples transformed completely. I began making new friends and exploring the city on my own, visiting Piazza Bellini, Via dei Tribunali, Via San Gregorio Armeno, Castel dell'Ovo, Cappella Sansevero, and the catacombs of San Gennaro. The locals were incredibly friendly, always smiling and giving compliments. The food, too, was even more delicious than in Rome. Surprisingly, Naples quickly became a city I adored, even more than Rome. While I cherish Rome for its art and history, my love for Naples grew because of its people. They were exceptionally welcoming, warm, and knew how to enjoy life. It's remarkable that on the first day, I was hesitant to walk the streets, but by the third day, the people of Naples had become my favorites.

No matter if it's a local or someone from another place who makes you fearful, don't adopt their fears. Stay mindful of your surroundings, but avoid letting fear dictate your actions or alter your plans.

Avoiding negative thoughts isn't sufficient on this journey. You should also find things to increase your excitement and nourish your dreams, especially regarding solo travel. After my first solo travel experience, I specifically shared my travel plans with individuals who wouldn't fill my mind with frightening scenarios and kept these plans a secret from others. I joined a Facebook group exclusively for female travelers, who shared amazing stories that kept me focused on my travel plans without any fear. Meeting solo travelers in Rome and hearing their stories further convinced me that solo traveling is feasible for anyone, regardless of gender. This is how I discovered the motivation to explore the world.

I'd advise you to do the same. Avoid discussing your travel plans with those who believe solo travel is boring or unsafe and who can't back up their statements with facts. Instead, share your ideas with people who can offer encouragement, and consider seeking inspiration from experienced groups, influencers, or authors of books that support your desired journey.

Four years after my South America trip, I met a 35-year-old Canadian girl, Jessica, in a hostel in Portugal. She had quit her job to travel Europe. As we discussed our travels, I mentioned my solo backpacking trip in South America. She expressed surprise and raised concerns about safety, language barriers, and finding people her age.

I shared my experience of initially traveling with no Spanish skills but later taking a two-week course to enhance communication. I assured her that it significantly improved my journey and even saved my life. I gave her the contact information of my Spanish teacher in Sucre, Bolivia. I emphasized that solo travel in South America, even for women, isn't as scary as it may seem. To ease her worries, I recounted positive stories and shared that I started my solo travels at 29, often meeting people younger than me without any issues. I invited her to a party that night, and we spent more time together, exchanging more travel stories.

Four months later, she posted a photo of her with my Spanish teacher in Bolivia, thanking me in her Instagram story. When we reconnected, she shared the unfolding events in her life and how my words had transformed her perspective, motivating her to pursue her dream. She spent several months exploring South America before returning home. In our subsequent conversations, she repeatedly conveyed her appreciation for my encouragement.

She simply required a boost from someone, although she already possessed the capability to embark on her travels independently. Just like the guy from Naples encouraged me. So, find people who cheer you on or find it within yourself to chase your dreams. Stay away from negative folks.

You might think that nobody can affect you. You might even have high trust in yourself. But believe me, people can plant fears in your mind, and suddenly you might find yourself scared of things you had never thought about. Two years later, after chatting with that Canadian girl, I felt the urge to explore South Africa. As I shared my plans, folks started giving me advice, even though I didn't ask. They warned me about the dangers, and it came from both a local and someone who'd recently visited. The local said it's unsafe for outsiders and suggested going with someone. The traveler talked about poverty, rape issues, and said I shouldn't go out at night. Despite having traveled to many places and feeling pretty confident, their words got to me. I decided to skip this month-long trip across South Africa.

A few weeks later, I bumped into an old friend. We chatted about my New Year plans, and I mentioned my idea to go to South Africa but how I'd changed my mind. She reminded me of the fearless adventurer I used to be. "Yasemin," she said, "you've tackled many 'dangerous' places and loved every bit. Just go for it, and if things get tough, you'll figure it out. There's always a way. You have been talking about South Africa for years. Everyone's different; maybe you'll really like it."

Her words hit home, and I decided to give South Africa a shot, even if just for a week. Turns out, it was incredible. South Africa welcomed me with open arms, and Cape Town, in particular, was enchanting. Everywhere I went—cafés, restaurants, supermarkets—people greeted me with smiles and friendly inquiries about my well-being. They offered city recommendations and safety tips, which is why I relied on Uber most of the time. The Uber drivers were delightful, engaging in fun conversations about South Africa, African music, and even Turkey. I felt warmly welcomed by everyone I met.

I took a cooking class and hiked Table Mountain, where all the guides were exceptionally kind. One of them even follows me on Instagram now, and I look forward to another hike with him on my next visit. In a shop selling paintings, the owner struck up a conversation about art, making my visit memorable. At the museum, I shared pleasant, smiling eye contact with everyone around me, and the same happened on the streets.

Dining in a restaurant in front of Camps Bay Beach, I had the best seafood. The restaurant owner, the bartender, and everyone else were incredibly nice, and I had enjoyable, brief conversations with each of them. It's rare to travel somewhere and have meaningful interactions with everyone you meet, where people smile at you and make you feel genuinely welcome all the time. Yet, in Cape Town, this was the norm.

This journey, much like my first trip to Rome, reminded me of my true self. From day one, I secretly hoped my return flight would get canceled, allowing me to stay longer. Cape Town, with its friendly people and stunning nature, captured my heart in an unexpected and profound way.

After this eye-opening adventure, I decided to put pen to paper in the form of this book. I want to dispel the fears that others may plant in your mind because most of them are not real. Fear grows as it is shared, and when we hear that someone else's fear originated from someone else, it's like a snowball effect. We need to be aware of this and not adopt anyone's fear.

CHAPTER

FOUR

THE TRUTH ABOUT SOLO TRAVEL AGE

When I embarked on my first solo travel adventure at the age of 29, most of the people I encountered during that trip were older than me, and I had so much fun with them. By the time I was traveling in South America at the age of 30, I noticed a shift where I became one of the older individuals, yet I continued to have a great time.

The people I spent time with were of different ages—some were 20, some were 26, some were my age, some were in their 40s, and some in their 70s. I never felt any age-related issues, and I'm sure they didn't either because the focus was on enjoying the moment. When we travel, we want to make each moment valuable, living in the present, and concentrating on having fun. Age becomes inconsequential.

In Peru, I met a guy who was 18 years old, already completing a one-year travel journey back to his home in the Netherlands. Meeting someone who was 18 years old and had already traveled more than me didn't make me feel old at 30; instead, I was happy that I was finally making it. Hearing his experiences and learning tips from a teenager was fascinating; I found him more mature than me, and it was a lot of fun.

In Sucre, I spent time with a woman who was probably 15 years older than me, although I never asked. We had a great time, and she even invited me to have tea with her 70-year-old mother on her birthday. Trying to converse in Spanish, we covered a lot, and I learned many things about local life, thoroughly enjoying the experience.

In Buenos Aires, I met a woman at least 10 years older than me. She was part of a band in the United States and was planning to meet with her band to play in a festival in Rio de Janeiro. She invited me to the hostel where she would be staying in two weeks. She has a truly unique personality and remarkably open-minded, humanistic views on society. It was so interesting to listen to her, talk about anything, and eventually hear her band on the streets of Rio de Janeiro. She was super fun too. We went to some festivals together, and she was wearing a banana costume so everybody wanted to take a photo with her. And five years later, we met in Paris. I have been talking to her and will see her again. She is one of my friends now.

During all my travels, there were people from different ages and cultures, and we all were happy to spend time together and have fun. Age was never an issue until I moved to Europe. At 33, people were often surprised by my age because I look significantly younger than I am, usually by about 8 years, as people often say. However, when they learned my actual age, some would exclaim, "Oh, you're old." Simply because I was a few years older, I was deemed old. Too old. They were even surprised about the muscles that I have in my 30s. The notion that people in their 30s are considered old by those in their 20s, and those in their 40s by those in their 30s, and so on, perpetuates this cycle.

After a while, I found myself influenced by the opinions of others, questioning whether I could still connect with young people who might perceive me as old. At that time, I was planning a trip to Costa Rica, and the idea of staying in hostels with predominantly younger crowds started to feel daunting. I began searching for accommodations catering to people in my age group, hoping it might be more comfortable, but I couldn't find any specific places tailored to my age. Eventually, I booked a hostel based on comments suggesting a mixed age range. In the hostel, I spent some time separately with people of different age ranges, but mostly, we were all together. We went out dancing, and the ages in the group ranged from 43 to 20, with me at 33. I had a fantastic time, reminiscent of how I enjoyed my previous trips too. It dawned on me how unnecessary it was to limit myself based on a couple of people who labeled me as "old." I was enjoying myself, and anyone who wanted to share in that was welcome. Likewise, if someone wished to share their enjoyment, I was more than willing to join in. Nobody cared about age.

So, even someone like me, who has traveled to many countries and had numerous positive experiences, can be influenced by other people's opinions and start questioning my age. You might feel the same way too. But believe me, when you're traveling, you won't dwell on your age or that of others.

Whether you feel old or not, you might be concerned about not meeting people in your age group. You're not alone in this worry; many solo travelers have similar thoughts. Therefore, search for hostels that cater to people in your age range and look for activities where you can meet individuals of your age. For example, if you choose club activities, you might find younger participants, but if you opt for hiking, you'll likely encounter an older crowd. Similarly, surfing, cooking classes, sightseeing buses, and free city tours tend to attract an older audience.

This is based on my experiences, and of course, yours may differ. This is your journey, and you will discover what you enjoy and find people to share those moments with. And it's your choice not to see age as a disadvantage but as an advantage. You might be more self-aware and attuned to your surroundings. You might travel more safely than someone younger and have a better understanding of your preferences.

Don't forget, age is simply a number, and should not be a limitation. The only limit is our beliefs. Whenever you are ready, it is the perfect time to pursue your desires. Anyone can travel at any age, and there are always people of your age looking to connect. When you travel, you will find them. Even if you don't, you will still enjoy your journey. I promise.

FIVE

CRAFTING YOUR TRAVEL ADVENTURE

DECIDING WHERE TO GO

Everyone travels in different ways. However, if you always travel with others, you might not fully discover what brings you the most joy. When we have companions, we often seek common interests, but these may not necessarily align with our personal preferences for maximum enjoyment. Traveling solo provides the opportunity to explore and uncover activities that truly bring joy.

If you've never had the chance to identify your preferences, making a plan may seem challenging. At this point, the importance of self-discovery comes to mind. Earlier, I mentioned finding activities that we enjoy. When we know our preferences, it becomes easier to decide where to go. That's why you should spend time and uncover your interests. However, sometimes, even though you know your interests, it might be difficult to decide where to go and how to make a plan.

If you're unsure, begin by touring countries that pique your interest. Search for activities each country offers, and then choose one that aligns with your preferences. For example, Rome was my initial choice due to my fascination with art and history; it boasts numerous museums and captivating sightseeing opportunities. Italy, in general, held many cities of interest for me, so on my first solo trip, I decided to explore Rome and Florence. Identify your own interests and, based on them, select a city or country for your solo travel adventure.

MAKE YOUR OWN PLAN

Once you've decided on the country you want to visit, the next task is creating a detailed plan, which may feel like the most challenging step. This phase requires dedicated time to make a list of your preferences, from places to visit to activities you'd like to do. The numerous choices might seem overwhelming, but don't worry—I have a reliable approach to share with you.

Instead of making strict plans beforehand, I created a simple method for easier decision-making. I made a flexible roadmap that outlined my goals for each country. The approach is unique for everyone. You will create your own roadmap and enhance the enjoyment of travel planning.

When I landed in Peru, the next day I googled activities to do in Peru and then must-see places in Peru, and so on. Then I wrote notes about them on my phone. It was a huge list and I could not decide what to do and where to go first. It might be the same for you too. Of course, there are must-see things such as Machu Picchu, but what about other options? I could not see everything in the country, so I had to pick a few of them.

I began by drawing a horizontal line across the center of an empty paper, essentially creating my own map with Peru represented. Since Lima is situated on the central western coast of Peru, and I was in Lima at the time, I checked its location on the map. Placing the horizontal line in the middle of the country, I marked a dot at the midpoint of the bottom of the paper to represent Lima, and then labeled it as such. Next to the dot I wrote activities that I want to do in Lima. Not all of them, but the must-do ones for me.

After adding Lima and the must-do activities there, I started to think about another must-see in the country: Machu Picchu. To get to Machu Picchu, I would need to go to Cusco. I checked Cusco on the map, and noticed it was close to Lima. I added another dot to my map. This dot was positioned close to the horizontal line and towards the right side of the paper, mirroring its geographical relationship as depicted on the map. Then I wrote about must-do activities in Cusco, such as hiking Machu Picchu and Rainbow Mountain.

Then I checked other cities and must-do activities and put dots for each of them on the map. At the end I saw that most of the activities that I was interested in were close to the right bottom side of the paper. There were other things that I was interested in on the left side of the paper, but most of them were on the right. So I decided to go to Cusco after Lima, then Arequipa and/or Puno.

The paper was like a road map for me. It was okay to change my mind on the way, if I heard of a new place to see, but I had a general idea about what to do in Peru. After Peru, I went to Bolivia because it was close, and my own road map automatically led me there. When I arrived in Bolivia, the very next day, I repeated the same planning process for that country. I chose the specific cities I wanted to explore in Bolivia.

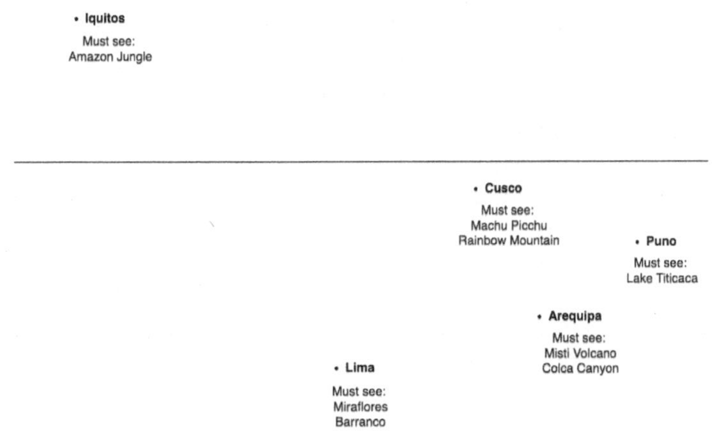

This practice is especially useful for those engaged in long-term travel, as it helps in deciding where to go within the country. Importantly, you don't have to wait until you arrive to make these decisions; planning in advance is an option. This approach worked well for me during my months-long backpacking journey when I preferred not to have a comprehensive plan initially.

For short-term trips, it is advisable to create a map before your travels. However, whether you're traveling for a short or long time, crafting your own map not only solidifies your plans but also allows you to seamlessly add additional cities as you go.

If you recall, when I was in Colombia heading to Santa Marta, I met some guys who were going to Palomino for tubing. I decided to join them because Palomino was still along my route, even though it was two hours away in the opposite direction. However, if it had been in a different part of the country, I wouldn't have gone, as most of the activities I wanted to do were in the current region.

After deciding which cities to visit in the country based on my must-see/do activities in each, I focused on each city individually. Since the must-do activities were limited, and there were more things to explore in the city or nearby areas, I always looked for enjoyable ones. Considering my passion for dance, I made sure to check out local clubs and searched for noteworthy restaurants and museums. I recorded these details on my phone, marking each location on my Google Maps. It's essential to mention that I didn't include these extra details on the initial paper map since its main purpose was to help me decide on destinations within the country. Once the decisions were made, the paper map became unnecessary.

If you already have a specific city in mind, you can forget the paper map and proceed to define the specific places you want to visit, eat, dance, etc., adding them directly to your personal Google Maps.

As you probably know, Google Maps allows you to save places and add a pin for each of them. I use this feature to mark every place I want to visit in a city. I assign the "Want to go" label for each place (museums, restaurants, squares), and for hostels or hotels, I use the "Favorites" label. This distinction makes it easy to identify places versus accommodations when looking at Google Maps. The "Want to go" label is green, and the "Favorites" is a pink heart, facilitating quick recognition when searching for accommodations. If I like a place after visiting, I change the "Want to go" label to a "Starred place." This way, on future visits to that city, I know my favorite places.

Additionally, when I mark a place to see on the map, I always include a nearby restaurant or café. This way, I don't need to search when I am there. I already know that there is a local option for food, which I had marked earlier.

STRATEGIES FOR FLIGHT BOOKINGS

When I decided to go to Peru, I was in Madrid. While it was certain that South America was my destination, the exact city or country remained undecided. The thought of experiencing Machu Picchu as my primary destination in South America influenced my decision to head to Peru first. A quick check on Skyscanner revealed budget-friendly one-way flights to Lima, prompting me to purchase a ticket from Madrid to kickstart my South American adventure. If you plan to embark on long-term travel for months and are uncertain about the countries to visit and the duration of your trip, follow the same approach: opt for a one-way ticket to the most cost-effective destination. Then, travel within the country using buses or trains, as they are often the most economical options. If you've meticulously planned and prefer a fixed itinerary, you can purchase a return flight from the last city you intend to visit.

If your travels are limited to a single country, once you've mapped out your journey on a paper map like the one I shared earlier, it's time to search for flights. At this point, you know which cities you want to visit. Begin by checking round-trip tickets to the capital, as flights are often more affordable for capital cities. Next, compare the costs between round-trip tickets to the capital and one-way tickets from your home to the initial city and then from the final city back home. This comparison will help you identify the more cost-effective option.

If your goal is to visit a single city, obtaining round-trip tickets from your home country to the destination is straightforward.

Unfortunately, I can't provide advice on finding cheaper tickets because those options are constantly changing. You'll need to conduct research each time. However, I can share the tools I use. Typically, I rely on Skyscanner to find affordable flight tickets, and occasionally I turn to Google Flights. Google Flights offers a map feature that allows easy exploration and comparison of various choices. For instance, you can select cities on the map and check for different routes to your destination.

When I decided to travel to Japan, my initial step was to search for the most budget-friendly city to fly to from Berlin using Skyscanner. Since I was residing in Berlin, the options it suggested from Germany were all priced over 1000 euros. Then, I turned to Google Flights, which recommended different ones. With Google Flights, I manually checked each country, searching for the most economical choices. To give you an idea, I checked tickets from Paris to Tokyo or Paris to Osaka, focusing on those two cities as potential starting points. I repeated this research for Madrid, Berlin, Frankfurt, and Copenhagen. Ultimately, I discovered a cheaper direct flight from Copenhagen to Tokyo. After identifying the airline, I visited its web page, searched for a flight from Berlin to Tokyo, and found an option that involved a one-hour flight from Berlin to Copenhagen, a two-hour layover, and then a direct flight to Tokyo. The total cost was 750 euros.

While Skyscanner and Google Flights show affordable options, sometimes they don't combine them to offer the cheapest itinerary. Therefore, it's crucial to delve deeper and conduct your own research.

STRATEGIES FOR ACCOMMODATION

After securing your flight tickets, the next step is to arrange accommodation. Here are a few considerations:

If you prefer not to plan your entire trip in advance and are unsure about the duration of your stay in a city, consider booking accommodation for the first two days only. This allows you the flexibility to decide on your plans once you're there. I've found that there are always available options, and last-minute bookings are often not significantly more expensive than if made earlier. Whether I'm on a long-term or short-term journey, I never reserve a hotel or hostel for more than two days. This approach offers the flexibility to change accommodations if needed, whether due to preferences or alterations in travel plans.

Once, for a short trip to Costa Rica lasting two weeks, I booked a round-trip flight to San José. My only plan was a two-day reservation at a hostel in San José. While I had a road map and key locations marked on my Google Maps—cities like La Fortuna, Santa Elena, Tamarindo, Montezuma, Puerto Viejo, and Quepos—I hadn't decided on the order of visiting. Arriving in San José at night, my initial plan was to explore the city the next morning. However, the next day, I encountered two fellow travelers in the hostel making plans to go to La Fortuna in just two hours. Engaging in conversation with them, I discovered they weren't particularly fond of San José. Since La Fortuna was on my list and I enjoyed their company, I decided to join them despite having already paid for that day at the hostel. It was a minor expense, and I quickly booked another option in La Fortuna. This spontaneous decision not only led to exploring La Fortuna but also other cities together. One of them became my travel companion.

For the remaining cities, I continued the pattern of booking accommodations for no more than two or three days, adjusting based on my interest and how much time I wanted to spend in each location. This flexible approach worked well, allowing me to extend my stay if I liked a place or easily find alternatives if needed, especially with hostels that usually have high turnover and available spaces, or nearby options. So, for greater flexibility, consider booking the initial two days and making your decision thereafter.

If your travel plans involve a single city, it might be practical to book your entire stay in advance, aligning each reservation with your budget. You can choose between hotels and hostels, or even a combination of both. During my visit to Cape Town, a short six-day trip, I decided to split my stay. I booked the first three days in a guest house that felt more like a boutique hotel. Anticipating the possibility of wanting a change in atmosphere, I reserved the following three days at a hostel. This way, if I ever felt the need for more social interaction, I knew the hostel environment would provide that opportunity.

However, if meticulous planning aligns better with your travel style, you might prefer to book your entire stay in advance. This approach allows you to focus on enjoying your trip without worrying about finding accommodations later. Additionally, having your accommodations sorted ahead of time can provide peace of mind and ensure you stay in places that meet your preferences and anticipated happiness levels.

Concerning the choice of tools, I always make my reservations using platforms like Hostelworld and Booking.com, making comparisons on both to secure the best deal. These platforms provide varying prices for the same option, so it's advisable to conduct a thorough search. Occasionally, I explore Airbnb as an alternative, but in my experience, it tends to be pricier.

Choosing between a hostel, hotel, or Airbnb depends on what you're looking for. If you want a calm and private vacation, a hotel or Airbnb might be better. But if you want to meet people and have an adventurous time, hostels are great, especially if you're traveling alone. The primary reason many people opt for hostels is to connect with fellow travelers.

Maybe some of you are concerned about safety in hostels, but they're generally safe. I even find them safer than hotels because the majority of guests are usually young travelers seeking a good time. On the other hand, hotels can be less predictable because anyone of any age could be staying in the room next door. As for Airbnb, although it's popular, I have some security worries because you're staying in someone's private home. Additionally, in some countries, Airbnb is not legal, making it crucial to rely on reviews and trust in the platform's safety measures.

Cleanliness is something to think about too. Surprisingly, I find hostels cleaner than hotels because they clean more often due to many guests. In hotels, I sometimes notice dusty rooms, making it unclear when they were last cleaned.

Another reason to prefer hostels is the opportunity to engage in various activities. Many hostels offer budget-friendly options for excursions through agreements with local tour providers, often cheaper than what you might find online. For this reason, I prefer to refrain from booking activities in advance and instead opt to book upon my arrival at the hostel.

The significance of exploring local choices extends beyond just considering the price. Gathering details and assessing alternatives is valuable. Internet searches can sometimes miss certain options, whereas in hostels, the staff can provide explanations, or fellow travelers may recommend superior alternatives, enhancing the overall decision-making process.

Take my experience in Cape Town—I had three hiking excursions in mind before arriving but decided not to book in advance. When I got there, I asked locals about hiking, and they recommended the best trails, considering weather conditions. One top suggestion was India Venster, and they advised waiting to check the weather. Considering the conditions, I booked a tour for a sunny day using Airbnb, and the price was the same as if I had booked in advance.

Following local advice on India Venster was a good call; it involved challenging rock climbing but offered unique sights not found on other paths. If I had pre-booked a different route, I might not have enjoyed it as much, and I wouldn't have factored in weather conditions like wind and sun. Hiking in Cape Town taught me that wind, especially, can be so strong that hiking becomes impossible. So, my advice is to consider and book activities in the city upon your arrival, especially if you're staying in a hostel where you might find others to join you.

~◈~

If you decide to stay in a hostel, it's crucial to choose one that aligns with your expectations since there are numerous options available. Start by exploring the most popular ones in the city, usually recognized by the highest number of reviews. Check the top three on platforms like Hostelworld and evaluate their locations on the map. Even if you ultimately decide not to book a hostel, this process helps you identify the most popular and tourist-friendly areas in the city. Hostels are often strategically placed in central locations for easy access to attractions. This is particularly important for solo travelers, as safety and the opportunity to connect with other travelers are significant considerations.

Checking reviews is a crucial step in this process. Both Booking.com and Hostelworld provide the age range of reviewers, offering insight into the demographic that typically stays at the hostel. Choosing a hostel popular among your age group can enhance your experience, as shared interests are likely. However, keep in mind that age doesn't always dictate compatibility; I've had enjoyable interactions with people younger/older than me who brought a lot of fun and enthusiasm to our shared activities.

Apart from the age range, you can also read about people's experiences. If there's a red flag for you in the reviews, you might consider skipping that hostel. However, don't discount a hostel just because of one bad review, as there will always be someone who isn't satisfied. Instead, compare the number of positive and negative reviews to make an informed decision about your stay.

Always check the pictures of the common areas in hostels before making a reservation. The main area is where people usually gather, sitting on couches and chatting about their day, and more. This communal space often becomes a hub for making new friends and forming plans together. If you enjoy socializing, opt for hostels with a lively main area. While some hostels have their own restaurants or cafés, which can be convenient, they may limit spontaneous interactions. So, having a vibrant main area is a good aspect to consider.

If you prefer a good night's sleep in your hostel room, avoid selecting a hostel with a bar or one known for hosting parties. Reading reviews can give you insights into the hostel's atmosphere; some hostels are celebrated for lively, all-night parties. If that's your preference, go for it—you're likely to enjoy the vibrant atmosphere. However, if a restful night is a priority, steer clear of party hostels.

Hostels typically offer three types of rooms: private, female-only, and mixed dormitory. During my travels in South America, I consistently opted for mixed dormitories due to their affordability. However, for subsequent journeys, I started choosing female-only rooms. This shift was prompted by my observation that mixed dormitories often have an unpleasant odor and are mostly dirty. Sometimes, the smell was so strong that it took a long time to get used to it and fall asleep. Unfortunately, this was my experience, as some male guests neglected personal hygiene.

Another option is a private room in the hostel. While it can be pricier, if you prefer having your own space, it's a worthwhile choice. Opting for a private room in a hostel can be a more affordable alternative to a hotel. Plus, it allows you to sample the hostel environment and provides opportunities to socialize with fellow travelers. It's a good way to get a taste of the communal atmosphere while still enjoying some privacy.

STRATEGIES FOR PACKING

When I began my first big journey, I had a sizable backpack weighing almost 50 pounds. On my first attempt to wear it, the backpack was so heavy and large that I couldn't put it on my back without sitting on the ground. While in Naples, a fellow Couchsurfing enthusiast recommended naming my bag, given its size was comparable to that of a human. I named it "Rome," symbolizing the starting point of my travel journey.

After a month or two, I became skilled at carrying the heavy backpack, but it remained a challenge for me. Being a budget traveler involved frequent walks, bus rides, and even hikes to reach hostels atop hills with the heavy backpack, making me wish for a lighter one each time. I even threw a few T-shirts in the garbage and cut my beach towel in half to make it smaller. Nevertheless, I completed my eight-month journey with that heavy backpack and then returned home. Afterward, I decided to invest in a smaller backpack for my future adventures. Regardless of its contents, it never exceeded 22 pounds, often staying around 15 pounds. This made hiking, walking, or moving around much easier.

Somehow, my small backpack carried more clothes than other travelers' big backpacks, all thanks to mastering the art of packing. The secret lies in the size of your clothes, not in their quantity. I invested in a thin, waterproof, and windproof jacket that doesn't take up much space. Alongside that, I have a thin sweater that keeps me warm without occupying too much room. Opting for thin towels suitable for the beach and personal use further maximized space. I also chose small skirts that don't wrinkle easily and a collection of versatile T-shirts.

With the new backpack I can accommodate clothes for a maximum of two weeks, but if I extend my travels, I can wash and reuse them every two weeks, which proves sufficient. The key strategy is to wear a fresh T-shirt or top daily, while bottoms, such as shorts or leggings, can be worn multiple times before washing. They don't occupy as much space as pants. So, choose clever items.

I transitioned to acquiring small, thin, yet highly practical items, and it has truly been a life-changing choice. You'll discover how much easier things become when you travel with fewer possessions but more utility.

Other than clothes, I always carry a power bank with me wherever I go. In hostels, it can be challenging to find available sockets, and they might be in use when you need them. Additionally, during activities like hiking, you may need to recharge your phone on the go, so invest in a power bank with ample capacity to charge multiple times. Also, consider purchasing a universal plug and keep it in your travel bag. This way, you won't have to deal with different plug types in countries using various socket standards.

If you're planning a long-term journey, consider packing a clothesline in your backpack. I would secure it to the bunk where I slept in hostels, enabling me to dry my underwear and socks. Since it was discreet, my hanging clothes didn't attract much attention. This practice proved to be a lifesaver. Regardless of how many pairs you have, keeping them clean on a daily basis is crucial, eliminating the need to wait until the next laundry day. For budget travelers, this not only ensures cleanliness but also becomes a key money-saving strategy. Washing your clothes by hand daily, including underwear, socks, and T-shirts, and letting them dry on the same day, eliminates the need for laundry services. While most hostels/hotels provide hand soap, carrying a small amount of laundry soap can be very useful. It's a simple yet effective way to save money. However, if you're on a short-term journey, this might not be necessary.

Another essential thing for long-term travelers is having a needle and thread.

If you have an old phone, consider placing it in your backpack as a backup in case you lose your primary phone.

Another indispensable item is a waterproof backpack cover, which not only protects your clothes from rain but also keeps your backpack clean.

Of course, there are many things to consider, but these are the essentials. The rest depends on your backpack size and personal needs.

BUDGET TRAVEL MASTERY

I had always dreamed of traveling the world, but thought it was impossible. Though I haven't traveled the entire world yet, I no longer consider it impossible. Because there is always another way and I have seen it.

Before deciding on my first solo trip, I had some credit card payments that needed attention. Traveling never crossed my mind because my salary was low, and everything seemed prohibitively expensive, especially considering the devaluation of the Turkish lira. Even though it was relatively better back then, it still wasn't valuable enough, especially for European travel. However, when I made the decision to visit Rome, I explored numerous options and settled on staying in hostels. This choice turned out to be a lifesaver as hotels in Rome were beyond my budget. Without this possibility, I might have accumulated additional credit card debt.

Visiting Rome as a budget traveler revealed to me that I could explore the world, or at least a part of it to start. My belief was not unfounded. I traveled for more than seven months; it all depends on our limits and standards.

In Europe, I chose hostels and utilized Couchsurfing to cut down on accommodation costs. Despite adopting a backpacker lifestyle, I continued to dine at restaurants, visit bars, and frequent museums, which could be quite expensive. And guess what? Everyone I met in Europe was traveling just like me.

When I arrived in Peru, I confronted reality—my money was depleting rapidly. Nearly half of my savings had vanished in just 40 days. Growing anxious, I sought alternative solutions. Before embarking on this journey, I had discovered a website called Workaway and decided to leverage it to cut down on accommodation costs.

Workaway connects local individuals with travelers. Locals post short-term job opportunities (ranging from one week to three months or more) on the platform, offering free accommodation and/or food. These jobs span various activities, such as assisting in farming, creating graffiti on a hostel's walls, conducting yoga classes, teaching English, or volunteering for organizations.

When I checked Workaway to find a job in Peru, all the available positions were pre-booked, requiring reservations at least a month in advance. Unfortunately, this made them unsuitable for last-minute decisions. I wanted to book something for my next destination, but plans were uncertain at that moment.

Consequently, I couldn't secure anything on Workaway. I knew many people who chose this platform and were thrilled with their travels. For them, Workaway became an integral part of their journey. They meticulously planned their travels, making reservations a month (sometimes three to four months) in advance, and then, based on their next Workaway destination, continued their journey. This approach didn't align with my preference. I wanted to go with the flow and avoid letting options dictate my choices. However, as mentioned earlier, it boils down to individual limits and standards. If you're interested, explore similar options on the Internet—there are likely numerous alternatives available now.

While I was still in Peru, I met a Brazilian guy, Felipe, after hiking Machu Picchu. He had been traveling in South America for a year with a bicycle. Staying in hostels, he earned money by offering his graphic design skills to local businesses. Unlike working continuously, he took on tasks in cities for a week or two, completed the job, and then moved on. I admired his approach because he didn't work throughout his entire journey.

As a software developer, it was challenging to find short-term jobs that aligned with my experience. So, I decided to explore alternatives. While staying at a hostel in Cusco that had its own bar, I noticed several foreigners working there on a short-term basis. I approached the owner of the bar and successfully secured a job for two weeks, which came with free accommodation, breakfast, and meal discounts. The job required only three days of work from 8 p.m. to 3 a.m.—it sounded both manageable and profitable.

On my first day, the hostel was buzzing with a lively party. I found myself behind the bar, skillfully crafting cocktails and joining in the celebratory bell-ringing that marked free shots for all bartenders. As the night progressed, I decided to decline further shots, but others insisted, creating an uncomfortable situation. That was the first thing that annoyed me. Then, some guys (again, bartenders) began behaving inappropriately towards the girls, including me. In response, I had to assert myself and make it explicitly clear that I wasn't comfortable with their actions. I even had to bend someone's finger. Only then did they stop disturbing me.

I don't remember how many cocktails I prepared; it felt never-ending. Finally, at 3 a.m., everyone left the bar except the staff, and I thought the night was wrapping up. The time had come to clean the bar, and they assigned me dishwashing tasks. Nobody mentioned it before. I washed millions of glasses, and managed to get to bed by 6 a.m., but my entire body was aching. Overthinking kept me from sleeping. I had quit my job not just to travel, but' to also avoid working the typical eight-hour day. I held strong views against capitalism and many societal norms, which still hold true. Working 10 hours on foot just to extend my stay in Cusco for a couple more days was too much, and not worth it. Consider this— if I worked three days until 6 a.m., for 10 hours each day, what could I do the next day? Just rest. While the accommodation and some meals were free, it didn't serve any purpose other than allowing me to linger a bit longer in Cusco. There was no extra money left for the next leg of my journey. That's when I realized that this type of traveling wasn't for me. It might be ideal for someone on a long-term journey, where travel becomes a way of life. They have the luxury of waiting and moving on to the next destination. In contrast, my mission was to live in the moment without being burdened by thoughts of money or work, simply focusing on the joy of traveling and enjoying life. After working one day, I quit that job at the bar in Cusco, and because I left two weeks earlier, they charged me for the night I stayed in the hostel. They didn't compensate me for the 10 hours of work. Without a contract, I had no means to assert my rights. At that moment, I found myself missing my previous job back home.

After that attempt, in Sucre, Bolivia, I decided on a different approach to working while traveling. I tried to secure a job in exchange for a Spanish course, offering my expertise in a familiar field (software development), making it more of a skill exchange than a traditional job. It turned out to be a more enjoyable experience compared to working in a bar.

Apart from these two instances, I hadn't actively sought employment during my travels. However, I encountered numerous fellow travelers who successfully combined work and exploration. Some of them not only enjoyed free accommodation but also earned money on the side. They offered classes like yoga, dance, and cooking in hostels, or engaged in creative activities like making graffiti. Their experiences seemed more rewarding and flexible compared to mine. If you have a skill you can share, consider giving it a try. It could open up new opportunities for both personal and professional growth during your travels and you can save some money to travel more.

Due to financial constraints and not having a job, I began planning ways to minimize my expenses. I opted for mixed dormitories where 10–12 people often shared a room, making it more cost-effective. To further reduce costs, I started cooking for myself—a game-changing decision. Supermarkets were readily available in every country, allowing me to buy affordable ingredients and prepare simple meals at hostels, most of which had fully equipped kitchens. South America, in particular, proved to be heaven for affordable and diverse food options. Meat, various vegetables, and fruits were all budget-friendly. Still, I was eating in some restaurants to sample the culture, but mostly, I was cooking for myself. I minimized my visits to clubs too. I was only going a couple of times in each country and especially to those that do not require an entrance fee. I even started boiling water instead of buying it, and I washed my clothes daily without incurring any cleaning costs. At the end, I managed to extend my travels to six and a half months with just half of my initial savings.

While my life became remarkably simple, I found myself happier than ever. I wasn't preoccupied with concerns about money or a job; instead, I focused on exploring and living in the moment. Happiness became uncomplicated now that life was simplified. I found joy in small things, like having a plug near my sleeping area or hot water in the hostel. I had never felt such profound emotion before. Whether it was hiking, dancing, or witnessing a sunset or sunrise, these experiences made me the happiest person.

You might think that minimizing your spending during travel would detract from your enjoyment. Or you might assume that staying in a luxury hotel would enhance your experience, and perhaps it does—I don't know you personally. However, the dilemma with hotels is that they often create higher expectations based on the amount of money spent. Even the highest-rated hotels receive negative comments from guests who expected more for the price they paid. The more we pay, the higher our expectations.

True enjoyment in travel, though, isn't necessarily tied to opulence; it's about moments, people, and simplicity. In simplicity, your expectations are low, and you're fully engaged. When you're not preoccupied with the pursuit of luxury, you can appreciate the little things, like a beautiful sunset, a friendly conversation, or a delicious street-food meal. These are the moments that create lasting memories and genuine satisfaction, proving that the best travel experiences often come from the simplest pleasures.

The real luxury is the ability to enjoy life in any condition, to believe in yourself and your capacity to thrive, no matter where you are. It's about letting go of the need for constant comfort and allowing yourself the freedom to embrace new experiences, whether they come from a five-star resort or a humble hostel. When you can find joy in the simplest of things and have the confidence to navigate the world on your own terms, that's when you've truly mastered the art of living richly.

Let me share a personal anecdote that illustrates this point.

Six months had passed since I started traveling, and I found myself in Tulum, Mexico, to meet with one of my friends, Mariana. I only had enough money for one month and decided to purchase my return flight to Turkey. However, most flights had layovers in the USA, Canada, or some European countries, requiring visas I didn't have. While there were direct flights from other countries, they were almost twice as expensive. Instead, I found a ticket from Cuba to Russia and from Russia to Istanbul, but the flights were two months later. With funds for only one month, I bought the tickets and resolved to spend less.

During this period, I started frequenting local eateries, opting for more pasta dishes. Tulum is known for being relatively expensive, but I managed to survive for one month, staying in the city center at a hostel rather than the upscale beach hotels. When Mariana joined, we stayed in an Airbnb room that didn't have hot water for showers. But that was okay since the weather was warm. We walked to the beach every day and sometimes hitchhiked. Despite having less money, we enjoyed coffee, had proper breakfasts, and relished delicious Mexican food at local spots. We went dancing at bars on the street, and everyone could join in the fun by just paying for a drink, which worked well for me since I didn't drink much. I had a fantastic time there, and one month later, I continued to Cuba. After Cuba, my journey ended, and I went back home to Istanbul.

The next year, after securing a job and saving some money, I decided to revisit Tulum and stay in one of the beachside hotels. As a budget traveler before, I felt like I had missed out on so many things in the fancier part of Tulum. I booked a luxurious hotel on the beach, but everything seemed off. The water was smelly, the room didn't meet my expectations, and I craved a brighter ambiance. Even though the beach was close by and accessible within minutes, it didn't bring the joy I had expected. The coffee wasn't as tasty, and everything felt different from what I had imagined. I was spending a significant amount of money, expecting a high level of happiness in return. Surprisingly, I had more fun when I was a budget traveler, because my expectations were low and everything was making me happy. And because I was a budget traveler, I had to go to local places more than before, making me discover more about the city. Mostly, those environments provide more socialization opportunities, so I met with many people while exploring the budget-friendly places. But, at my luxurious hotel, I felt so lonely and it was so difficult to socialize. To be able to have fun on my fancy holiday, every day I went to the city center that I had explored the previous year. So, I was able to enjoy more than the fancy part.

I learned that taking a luxurious trip doesn't necessarily make your travel experience better. While there are times when some of us may appreciate luxury, myself included, a lack of money doesn't mean you can't have fun or travel. In fact, the opposite is true—when you have limited funds and actively seek alternatives, those options can bring you more joy than anything else.

Having a small budget is no reason to avoid traveling; it's just an excuse. Every country offers various choices for budget travelers—we just need to decide based on our budget and priorities. If you can't travel for two weeks, why not try one? If hotels are too expensive, try hostels. If sharing a room isn't your preference, explore private rooms in hostels. If even hostels are out of reach, consider cheaper hotels. If dining out is too pricey, shop at supermarkets. Every country has supermarkets offering affordable and delicious home-cooked meals. If that's still expensive, try cooking for yourself—it's the most cost-effective option, and you'll likely find it enjoyable. Most hostels and many other accommodations have kitchens available. If transportation costs are high, consider renting a bicycle. Almost every country offers bicycle rentals for various activities. Or try walking. I've walked 25 kilometers in a day, and while it's tiring, the effort makes the destination more meaningful, and the sense of accomplishment upon arrival is incredibly rewarding. If you want to combine travel and work, numerous short-term jobs are available in every country; just remember to book in advance.

There is always an alternative; just give it a try with a short trip. Choose options based on your budget and see if you enjoy it. I am sure you will cherish every moment.

CHAPTER
SEVEN

THE PATH TO SAFE TRAVELING

PERCEPTIONS OF SAFETY

The perception of safety often depends on what others say, leading us to think we are safe just because it's labeled that way. However, in the same circumstances, without external assurances, we might feel unsafe. This dynamic highlights how others' opinions can significantly shape our beliefs about safety. That's why I'm generally skeptical about what I hear about safety from social media and the news.

For me, safety is relative and hinges on how society views crimes. If a society considers a certain type of crime acceptable, then, in my view, the country isn't safe. On the flip side, if committing a crime publicly is discouraged, and such activities have to be done privately, I consider that country trustworthy. This is how I define safety, and I believe it's a valid perspective.

In my country, Turkey, it's unusual for someone to steal from you openly. In our society, people actively avoid causing harm, and this is deeply rooted in our culture. In certain countries such as Saudi Arabia, United Arab Emirates, and Oman, individuals don't even lock their shops when going to a mosque because theft is rare due to cultural norms. If someone tries to steal, others in the community would step in to stop it. However, despite these cultural practices, news reports often portray the countries I mentioned as unsafe for travel. The reason for this might be political or for other reasons that I'm not really interested in. For me, these countries are safer than others where people do not look out for each other.

This perspective is further supported by the recent 2024 "15 Safest Countries to Travel in 2024" report published by Berkshire Hathaway Travel Protection, as highlighted by *Forbes* in an article by Brittany Anas, published on November 19, 2023. The list predominantly features European countries, with Canada topping the list, followed by Switzerland, Norway, Ireland, and the Netherlands. Brazil is also included at number 15, which surprised me in a good way. Despite some areas in Brazil being known for higher crime rates, it's encouraging to see it recognized for the safety it offers in many regions, especially in contrast to some countries that didn't make the list.

What's particularly striking, however, is the absence of any African or Middle Eastern countries, such as the UAE, Saudi Arabia, or Oman, where crime rates are so low that people often don't even lock their stores. For instance, Rwanda, with its impressive safety record and low crime rates, is often overlooked despite being safer than many European cities. This stands in stark contrast to cities like Paris and Barcelona, where theft is a common occurrence, yet these locations still feature prominently on the list of safest countries.

Moreover, even outside the Middle East and Africa, there are other examples, such as Singapore, which is renowned for its stringent laws and incredibly low crime rates. Yet, Singapore is absent from this list as well. This disparity highlights how safety is often perceived through a Western-centric lens, overlooking regions that may, in fact, offer a safer environment for travelers. For me, true safety is often found in places where community bonds are strong and people look out for each other—places that, unfortunately, do not always get the recognition they deserve.

I don't understand why, but whenever a country is poor, it's labeled as unsafe. Have you ever heard of a country that is considered rich but not safe (except for some Muslim-majority ones, which are often excluded from the safest country lists likely because of their religion)? Conversely, if it's rich, it's considered safe. This trend also applies within the same country. Poor neighborhoods are seen as unsafe, while rich ones are considered safe. People associate poverty with danger, but the truth is, those in less affluent neighborhoods often display more humanity, liveliness, and helpfulness.

When I decided to travel to South America, I kept It a secret from my father until just one month before my departure. I didn't want him to worry or feel sad for an extended period before my trip.

You know how fathers can be protective. This is especially true with Turkish fathers; it's part of our culture. They are incredibly protective and cherish their daughters a lot. At least, that's how it is in my family and where I grew up.

Upon learning about my plans, my father tried to convince me to limit my travels to Europe, just as I expected. His concern stemmed from the belief that South America isn't safe enough for travel, but how could he know? He had never traveled there before, and was simply going by what he'd heard from the news. News, where people's minds are filled with fake information. Luckily, he didn't express specific concerns related to safety for a woman, reflecting our family's commitment to equality. In our household, gender doesn't come with separate definitions. Perhaps that's why I strongly believe that if a country is unsafe, it poses a threat to both women and men. I don't buy into the idea that a country can be safe for men but not for women. Therefore, don't specifically search for countries safe for women on the Internet.

However, if a woman's goal is to travel without interference or obstacles, it's important to be selective about which countries you choose to visit based on your comfort level and personal preferences. Different cultures have varying attitudes and behaviors towards women, and what feels comfortable for one person might not be the same for another. To ensure a more enjoyable experience, consider researching the cultural norms and social expectations of your destination. This way, you can choose places where you'll feel most at ease and able to fully enjoy your travels.

Regarding my time in South America, numerous people expressed surprise at the fact that I, as a woman, was traveling alone, especially to South America. The majority of those who found it surprising were from Europe. But in South America, nobody was taken aback or shocked that I was traveling by myself or that I was a woman traveling alone. On the contrary, they offered more support and encouragement for my travels than anyone else. "Scary" South America was safer than anywhere else to me. I had no issues, encountering only help and kindness.

In reflecting on my experiences and the perceptions of safety across different cultures, it's clear that the label of "safe" or "unsafe" is often more about societal biases than reality. What we perceive as dangerous is frequently influenced by media narratives and preconceived notions, rather than actual experiences. My journey through South America, despite the concerns of others, taught me that safety is relative and often found in places where communities are strong and supportive, regardless of economic status or predetermined labels. As travelers, we should challenge these perceptions, remain open-minded, and recognize that true safety often lies in the unexpected—a friendly encounter in a so-called "dangerous" place, or the quiet reassurance of a community looking out for one another. Ultimately, it's about embracing the world with an informed yet open heart, trusting in the humanity that transcends borders, and finding your own sense of security in the connections you make along the way.

STORIES EXPOSING BIASES

I was buying a bus ticket to go to La Paz, Bolivia from Cusco, Peru. I asked the seller multiple times if the bus would drop me off at the main bus station in La Paz, and he assured me it would. I wanted to confirm this because the main bus station was close to the hostel I was headed to, making it easier for me to navigate without communication problems.

I bought my ticket and got on the bus. It was a 15-hour trip, but turned out to be more comfortable than a hostel, since the seats could be converted into beds. As we approached La Paz, a person not driving, but a guide of some kind, began announcing something in Spanish and handed out papers to everyone. Without Internet access, I couldn't search for information or understand what he was saying. Everybody seemed like a local on the bus, but I stood up and asked, "Is there anybody who can speak English?" That's when a guy started talking to me.

"I can speak English," he said.

"Oh, perfect. What did the guy say, and what are these papers? I don't understand anything," I said.

"We need to fill out these papers to pass the border. First, we'll stop at the Peruvian border to get a stamp for our passports, then board the bus. Afterward, it will stop at the Bolivian border, and we'll go through passport control. You'll need this paper during passport control."

"Okay. Can you help me fill out this form because I don't know Spanish?"

"Sure," he said.

That's how our conversation started. I learned that his name was Ethan, he was from Canada, and that he was a scientist conducting research related to water in Bolivia. I followed him through the border procedures, and we boarded the bus bound for La Paz. During the journey, the guide made another announcement, and Ethan started preparing to disembark.

"What's going on?" I asked Ethan.

"We need to get off here; it's the last station."

I looked around, but it didn't resemble a bus station. It looked more like a desert, with nothing in sight, not even a house.

"We just crossed the border. Are we in La Paz already? It doesn't look like a city center. Can you ask the guy if we're in La Paz?"

Ethan, busy with his luggage, didn't respond. I grabbed my handbag and followed him off the bus. We stood in front of it, while Ethan was talking to the guide.

"Hey, are we in La Paz?" I asked.

"This is the last station," Ethan said.

I turned to the guide and asked directly in English, "Are we in La Paz?" He didn't answer, just stared at me, then handed me my backpack from under the bus.

I kept asking, "Is this La Paz?" The guide reboarded the bus, and it started moving. Ethan and I were left outside.

I was becoming exasperated. "If this is the last station, why didn't anyone else leave the bus? And where is it going?"

"Sorry, maybe I was wrong," Ethan said. "Anyway, I need to go to the airport from here."

"Sorry?! Damnit! Because of you, I left the bus. If you weren't sure, why did you say it's the last station?"

I was stomping my feet because I was so angry that I had just believed him. Not bothering to wait for his answer, I grabbed my backpack from the ground, and started walking down the empty road, uncertain how I'd find a taxi in such a desolate place.

After walking for a few minutes, I came across a place with small buses and some people. Approaching one of the men, I showed him the hostel address from my phone. Unfortunately, nobody could speak or understand English. The man took my phone from my hand, showing the address to others while speaking in Spanish. Then, another man got off a bus we were standing in front of, took the phone, and gestured for me to sit next to him. Following his lead, we relied on body language for communication. Even though he spoke in Spanish, his gestures seemed to convey, "Sit here, we're going in that direction, and I'll help you."

It was a small bus, with some people sitting and others standing. Once it was full, it started moving. The man next to me held onto my phone and conversed with the driver throughout the journey. Behind me, there were two kids (around 10 to 12 years old) with a woman, likely part of his family. They occasionally talked, and the kids teased the man, sharing laughs at his remarks. My mind was preoccupied with cursing Ethan, so I wasn't concerned about the possibility of theft or being scammed. Somehow, I trusted the man; it was a gut feeling.

After two hours, we arrived at what seemed like a city center. During the ride, the man held onto my phone, people chatted on the bus, and the kids continued their laughter. Everyone else disembarked, leaving only me, the driver, and the man. The bus continued a bit further and then stopped. The man indicated the door, spoke to the driver, and we left the bus. The driver continued on his route.

The man showed me my phone but didn't return it. I didn't ask, either. He pointed to the address on the phone and communicated something. Then, he hailed a passing taxi, and we got in. During the ride, he spoke with the taxi driver, providing directions using the address. Five minutes later, the taxi halted. The man reached for money to pay the driver, but I intervened and covered the fare. I should mention that he had already paid for my bus ticket.

He then rang the doorbell of the hostel, and a staff member opened it. They spoke, and the man showed the address. Subsequently, I was able to converse with the staff member in English. It was the correct hostel, after all.

I turned to the man and said thank you. He expressed many things in Spanish, and surprisingly, I understood everything through his body language. He gestured towards my phone and advised me not to keep it exposed, emphasizing the potential danger of theft. He reassured me, saying, "Now I can go home in peace because you are in the right place."

Those were the words I grasped from his expressive gestures. I never learned his name. Without any knowledge of Spanish to inquire, I showed my gratitude with a simple "gracias." It was the moment when I decided to learn Spanish—not just to travel more easily but also to ask for people's names, engage in conversations, socialize with the locals, and, more importantly, say more than "gracias."

If you saw him and the other people on the small bus, it would be clear that all of them were poor. Despite this, the man was willing to pay for my bus fare and even for my taxi. He accompanied me to the hostel to ensure I arrived safely. Who would do that? People often label South America as unsafe, but I felt so secure there because of all the humans that I met. Yes, not just people, but humans.

During my time in La Paz, I explored the bustling Witches' Market, admired the Basilica of Saint Francis, and enjoyed the panoramic views from Mirador Killi Killi. I also visited the Coca Museum and the Museum of Musical Instruments. A highlight of my stay was a trip to Lake Titicaca and La Isla del Sol, which became my favorite spot. After spending a week in La Paz, I decided to travel to Sucre. I had heard about numerous Spanish teachers and schools there that were affordable. I hopped on another local bus, and during the ride, a woman, Mirtha, started conversing with me in English when she realized I was a tourist. She was from Sucre and worked as a lawyer. Though her English was limited, we managed to communicate. The journey to Sucre took around 10–15 hours. Once we reached Sucre, she walked with me from the bus station to the city center. We exchanged numbers and agreed to meet during my stay. She even invited me to her family's home, and when I left Sucre, she gave me a box of chocolate made in Sucre as a gift. We still keep in touch.

Upon reaching my hostel, I inquired about a Spanish course, but the offered price was a bit steep for my budget. Undeterred, I explored other options, but they were even more expensive. As a budget traveler without any income, everything seemed expensive. Then, while passing another hostel, I noticed a sign advertising Spanish courses. I inquired, and though it was the cheapest find, it was still beyond my budget. So, I approached the hostel owner and explained my situation. I offered to help with computer-related tasks since I am a software engineer, and in return, asked for a discount on the course.

She responded, "I can't offer a discount on the course as the teacher has a fixed price. However, I do need help with a website that was implemented by another traveler, and I don't know how to update things. If you can assist with that, you can stay in my hostel for free."

It was the best offer. I only had to pay for the Spanish course for two weeks. The next day, I left my current hostel and moved to the new one, where I started my first Spanish course—two hours of private lessons every day.

After the first class, I went to the reception and asked the owner, Gabi, what I could do for the website. She replied that it wasn't urgent and she would let me know later. A week passed, and she hadn't assigned me any tasks. Only once did she ask me to change a few pictures on the website. That was the extent of the work she gave me during those two weeks. In the end, I realized that she just wanted to help me, and she did so in the politest way. I initially thought we were doing business, but, in reality, she was simply offering help.

One day, we had the opportunity for a lengthy conversation. Gabi shared that she used to work as a Spanish teacher before opening the hostel. Initially, she had been saving money to buy a car. However, facing financial challenges, she opted for a stable job instead. Consequently, she invested the money into opening the hostel and started teaching Spanish there, collaborating with other Spanish teachers. At the time, the hostel didn't generate much income since it was new, and she was working hard to make it more popular. During our conversation, she expressed pride in my travels and encouraged me to explore more of South America. What struck me was that she never questioned how I managed to travel as a solo woman. It was a refreshing experience, as in South America, nobody seemed surprised by backpacking or solo travel, even for women.

While Gabi wasn't earning enough to cover her own expenses, she supported and encouraged my travels. Her assistance never felt like charity; it was given with genuine kindness. I wished to repay her more, but my financial situation was limited.

Do you remember Jessica, the Canadian girl that I met in Portugal? I shared Gabi's information with her and she took Spanish courses from her. Over the years, circumstances prevented me from returning, but I sent another traveler to her. Both Gabi and Jessica were delighted to connect. Gabi, despite living in one of the poorest countries, is truly one of the richest individuals in the world. Her passion for helping women and travelers makes her truly special.

I have many more stories about how local people helped me while I was traveling. One unique aspect across all of South America is the profound importance they place on travel. There's a deep respect for anyone exploring the region, and many aspire to embark on their own journeys someday. This shared sentiment often leads them to extend a helping hand to anyone traveling, creating a welcoming and supportive atmosphere.

I met a Chilean girl, Pia, in a hostel while I was in Peru, and within just two days, we became close friends. She graciously invited me to stay in her apartment if I ever visited Santiago. When I found myself in San Pedro de Atacama with a broken phone, I learned there was an Apple store in Santiago where I could get it repaired. I messaged Pia from my tablet, explaining the situation, and without hesitation, she welcomed me, saying I could stay for as many days as needed.

Upon arriving in Santiago, Pia picked me up from a bus station and assisted me in fixing my phone. I spent a wonderful week in her apartment, where she took me to tourist spots, showed me around, and introduced me to her friends. As I was leaving for Bariloche in Argentina, she unexpectedly gave me her winter jacket because I was traveling with summer clothes to Patagonia, where it could get cold.

Puzzled, I asked, "How can I give it back to you?"

Pia replied, "You don't have to. Just leave it in a hostel for someone else who needs it."

It was a brand-new winter jacket, and she simply gave it to me. Reflecting on the experience, I find it surprising because, as a software engineer, I used to earn a comfortable income before quitting my job to travel. Throughout my journey, the people I met earned less than me, and even though I didn't need assistance, they wanted to help me to encourage more travel with my savings. This unique culture of supporting others to explore more is something I've found particularly special in South America. Coming from Turkey, a country known for its hospitality, I'm familiar with inviting someone into your home and offering food, but the idea of helping others to travel more is truly extraordinary.

And there's more. I met three guys in Argentina, and one of them expressed his desire to support my journey of exploring the world with a limited budget. He offered his home for me to stay in if I ever visited Buenos Aires. Upon arriving at his place, he handed me a public transportation card already loaded for use, shared his food, and took me on a tour of the city.

These are just a few examples, and there are many more stories like these. What makes them extraordinary is that none of these people expected anything in return. They were genuinely happy to contribute to my travels and be a part of the experience.

People helped me in Brazil, Colombia, Mexico, Bolivia, and Argentina—countries often perceived as challenging travel destinations. Yet these are the very countries where I encountered some of the most compassionate and humane people.

Here is a text that I wrote and shared on Facebook after I traveled to Salvador da Bahia.

Smiling at the World

I am a person who always smiles; it's a part of my character. Today, I realized that because of my smile, I consistently meet wonderful people.

Today marked one of the most beautiful days of my trip. I was pleasantly surprised by the people from Salvador. They were incredibly charming and friendly. Who said Brazil is dangerous?

As I wandered around, a man called me over. When he learned that I had never watched capoeira, he graciously gave me a chair and started dancing. Then, a woman sitting with me, upon hearing that I had never tried coconut water, promptly ordered one for me. Another man gave me a gift (a handmade bracelet) and then unexpectedly hugged me. For an hour, we all engaged in a delightful conversation, and then I continued to explore the surroundings.

While walking, a guide approached and began explaining the history of the city. We hung out together for two hours. He treated me to coffee and introduced me to local people working on the street, all of whom warmly embraced me and said 'welcome.' I wanted to pay the guide for his services, but he declined.

On my way back, two men greeted me, and we struck up a conversation. They took my pictures, offered advice about the city, and we even danced together on the street. All of them mentioned that they liked my smile.

When I returned to the hostel and shared my day with others, I was surprised that they agreed people here are nice, but nobody experienced the same things I did. The hostel owner said it might be about me.

Now I understand why I've encountered wonderful people throughout my travels. It's because I love people, the world, life... and I always smile. When you smile, they smile too.

When people smile at each other, good things happen. Smile at the world :D. And look at the pictures; there is only one language: smiling :D

I don't know if I met all those nice people because I was smiling, or maybe it went both ways—I was smiling, and they were smiling too. If smiling makes it safer, then let's smile at the world.

THE CRUCIAL ROLE OF TOURISM OPTIONS

Leave all biases behind and shift your focus from solely worrying about safety to thinking about where you truly want to go. Don't let fear hold you back; there are countless solo travelers world-wide exploring even the so-called "dangerous" countries. Perhaps it's not as perilous as it seems, and what people often label as "dangerous" is, in reality, just poverty. I don't see these places as impoverished; for me, these are some of the richest countries because of their unique cultures. Embracing these cultures and stepping out of your comfort zone can lead to some of the most rewarding travel experiences.

Because I have never encountered any problems while traveling, I can't assert that the entire world is completely safe and nothing will happen. However, this doesn't imply that you will be in danger, or conversely, that you are entirely safe even in the world's safest country. My intention is to convey that perhaps the world is not as dangerous as some would like us to believe. It's important to do your own research and gather information from reputable sources, but ultimately, the decision of where to travel should be based on your own instincts and feelings. Trust yourself to make the right choice for you. If you feel confident and secure about a destination, that belief can enhance your experience. Conversely, if you approach a place with fear, that mindset might color your perception. Your intuition, combined with careful consideration, should guide your travel decisions.

While trusting your instincts is crucial, it's also helpful to recognize that a thriving tourism industry can be a strong indicator of a destination's safety. If a country has a well-established tourism sector, it is generally considered safe to travel. This is because both the government and the local communities have a vested interest in providing safer options to sustain and grow tourism. For instance, popular destinations often offer well-regulated tour operators, secure transportation choices, and accommodations with rigorous safety standards. These elements work together to create a safer environment for travelers. Therefore, you can always find a way to explore the city or country you want to visit by tapping into these resources.

Start by researching activities, tours, hostels, and transportation options specific to your destination. Many countries with rich cultures and histories have developed extensive tourism networks to ensure that visitors can explore safely. Look for local guides who know the area well, join group tours if you're traveling solo, and choose accommodations with good reviews from fellow travelers. These options not only enhance safety but also enrich your travel experience by connecting you with the local culture in a meaningful way.

Including travel advisories in your research ensures that you're aware of potential risks such as natural disasters, political unrest, or health concerns, allowing you to make informed decisions and avoid unnecessary hazards. For example, I found it risky to travel to Hawaii, Cuba, and the Caribbean during August and September because almost every year there is flooding due to hurricane season. Being aware of such details can help you avoid unnecessary risks and plan your travels more wisely.

As you continue to travel, you'll gain more confidence in navigating different environments. Each journey teaches you something new about how to stay safe and what to consider when choosing your next destination. Your awareness and instinct for safety will sharpen with experience, allowing you to take on more adventurous trips with greater ease. Over time, you'll find that your confidence grows, and you'll be more inclined to explore places that once seemed out of reach. Ultimately, travel is about more than just visiting new places—it's about growing your confidence, expanding your horizons, and embracing the richness of the world around you. With each journey, you'll learn that safety is not just about external factors but also about your own ability to navigate and enjoy the world with an open heart and mind.

SHIELDING YOURSELF FROM BECOMING A TARGET

Up until now, I've aimed to share that traveling is generally safe, and countries labeled as "unsafe" can indeed be "safe." You've heard a few stories about how people help and approach solo travelers, and it's not just me—there are numerous solo travelers with their own unique stories. Building on this positive perspective, let's shift the focus to discuss aspects that require careful consideration when we travel.

It doesn't matter whether you are in your own country or a different one, if you walk on the street appearing fearful, someone might perceive you as vulnerable. Projecting confidence is crucial to avoid unnecessary risks.

Once, I was on a metro in Italy when a man entered the carriage. A local girl was sitting in front of me, and the moment she saw him, she became visibly frightened. It wasn't his appearance that alarmed her—his clothes were ordinary—but rather his demeanor. He seemed to be on the lookout for someone to intimidate, his eyes darting around with an unsettling intensity as if he were sizing up potential victims. There was a menacing energy about him, as if he was just waiting for the right moment to lash out. He sat down next to her and began harassing her with words I couldn't understand. Despite her efforts to avoid eye contact and distance herself, her fear seemed to embolden him. Eventually, she was forced to get off at the next station. Strangely enough, as a tourist, I wasn't his target. Perhaps it was because her visible fear made her an easier mark. I sat up straight, projecting confidence, ready to meet his gaze if he approached. This is the kind of stance we should adopt while traveling.

Some people unintentionally display fear, which may attract potential harm. However, those individuals, like the guy, often lack the courage to confront someone projecting confidence. They tend to target those who appear more easily intimidated. Regardless of where you are, walk with confidence, as if you own the place, as if it's your own neighborhood, without showing fear. It boosts self-esteem and sends a signal that you won't be an easy target. Potential troublemakers are more likely to choose an easier mark.

Of course, there are people in the world who engage in pickpocketing, violence, and mugging. In a situation where someone has a gun or weapon and demands money, it's crucial to prioritize personal safety and to comply. However, the key is not to make yourself an easy target before they pick you. By projecting confidence and assertiveness, you are less likely to be victimized in the first place.

Once, while walking in La Boca in Buenos Aires, I sensed someone following me. Without hesitation, I abruptly turned back and confidently exclaimed, "¿Qué pasa? (What's up?)" It was a clear signal that I was aware and ready to address any issue. Caught off guard, he glanced at the sky, then turned away to walk in the opposite direction. This happened during the day, in a crowded area. He couldn't afford the risk. Taking a stand like this can deter potential troublemakers, making it less likely for you to become a target. Trust yourself and stride confidently through the streets you navigate.

Another time, I found myself in a favela, a type of slum or shantytown in Rio de Janeiro. Despite warnings against going alone, I decided to visit. I made sure not to take out my phone or snap any pictures, carrying only a small amount of money in my pocket. Dressed in a simple, formal skirt and shirt, I blended in without drawing attention. Walking confidently, I explored the area to observe real local life—how people lived and interacted. Intent on experiencing rather than capturing, I entered a store to buy açai, a personal favorite. There were a couple of people in the shop. Even though I knew Portuguese was expected, I used my limited Spanish to make my purchase, thinking they would understand that better than English. Realizing I was a tourist, the shop owner, though willing to accept my money, seemed unwelcoming. Sensing potential tension, I swiftly left the store and the neighborhood. My gut feeling told me I wasn't wanted there, and staying might lead to problems. It's crucial to listen to your instincts and, even when leaving due to potential issues, always approach with respect.

When I mention walking like I own the neighborhood, it doesn't imply exerting power over others. It means trusting yourself, avoiding any sign of weakness, and not making yourself an easy target. However, when you sense potential danger, leaving respectfully is crucial, but it's equally important not to show fear. In situations like the one in the favela, I couldn't assert myself with "¿Qué paso?" due to the man's attitude. Knowing when to stand your ground is essential.

ADDITIONAL FACTORS FOR SAFE TRAVEL

When it comes to safe traveling, accommodation is another crucial aspect to consider. I always prefer hostels because they are typically situated in safe and touristy areas. If you opt for a hotel or Airbnb, aim to find the most popular hostels in the area and select a location accordingly. Ensuring your accommodation is in a well-traveled and secure location can contribute significantly to your overall safety.

If public transport is deemed unsafe, consider using Uber or other options. Pay attention to recommendations from fellow travelers in hostels or hotels, as well as advice from locals. Take necessary precautions, but don't let fear dictate your journey. Opt for accommodations in tourist-friendly areas and, if safety is a concern, try to be outdoors during daylight hours.

I typically love exploring cities on foot and can walk up to 25 kilometers in a day. However, when I visited South Africa, I received warnings not to walk on the streets but to use Uber instead. I heeded the advice, avoiding unnecessary risks and opting to navigate the city that way. This decision allowed me to engage in meaningful conversations with Uber drivers, gaining insights into the city from their perspective. The choice of transportation should always be adapted based on the situation.

While I usually like solo hiking, concerns about safety in Cape Town led me to choose guided hikes with a group. The key is to listen to locals, take precautions, and pursue activities you enjoy, as every city offers various ways to explore, with safer options available. You'll likely discover these choices upon arrival. Have a chat with the hotel or hostel staff, as well as fellow travelers you meet; they are valuable sources for providing insights.

Another safety consideration involves money. While money is important, be prepared to potentially lose it at any time. If someone demands your money and you find yourself in a situation where you cannot protect yourself, it's advisable to hand it over, prioritizing your safety. However, always ensure that you have additional funds accessible. This is especially crucial for backpackers on long-term journeys. Avoid keeping all your money in one place; instead, separate it into different locations. Have multiple cards from different banks, each with different limits, and set low limits for added security. If somebody were to take your credit card, you know that its limit is low and you have other options. With advanced online banking features, such as defining daily limits, you can have peace of mind knowing nobody can use more than the limit, and you can always cancel the card.

Before I started traveling, I crafted two small cloth wallets and attached them with VELCRO® tape inside the cups of my bra. This discreet setup provided an extra layer of security for my belongings throughout my journeys. I distributed my money across five cards from two different banks: two debit cards and three credit cards. I placed one debit card and one credit card in each bra cup, with an additional card kept in my wallet. This ensured that if my wallet was ever stolen, I would still have backup options securely hidden elsewhere. Additionally, by spreading my funds across different bank accounts, I minimized the risk of being unable to access my money due to issues with a single account or bank. This redundancy is particularly important during long trips, as it gives you alternatives if something goes wrong. I never needed to access the cards in my bra while in public; instead, I planned ahead, choosing the card I would need and placing it in my wallet before heading out. When one account was depleted, I would swap the card from my bra with another, treating it like a personal vault. Creating hidden pockets within your clothing and strategically storing extra money or cards can greatly enhance your security while traveling.

During my travels in South Africa, I carried an extra phone in my backpack. Since my backpack was usually left at the hostel, the second phone served as a backup in case my primary phone was stolen. Despite its older model and a battery life of only one to two hours, the backup phone was a valuable asset, providing a lifeline in emergencies. It allowed me to connect to the Internet or make calls if I ever lost my primary phone. Fortunately, I never had to use it, but having a backup was a reassuring precaution.

Remember, every country has its risks, but that shouldn't deter you from pursuing your travel dreams. The key is preparation and awareness. By doing thorough research, listening to locals, trusting your gut, and carrying yourself with confidence, you can navigate even the most challenging environments. Start with well-known destinations to build your travel instincts and gradually expand your horizons, always refining your approach to safety. Taking precautions—like securely storing your valuables, planning your routes, and choosing destinations with a variety of tourism options—can empower you to explore the world without fear. Through these strategies, I've been able to visit some of the most extraordinary and welcoming places, turning potential dangers into unforgettable adventures.

I hope that by sharing these insights, I've shown you that with the right mindset and preparation, the world is yours to discover. So, if you have a dream destination in mind, don't let fear hold you back. Prepare, be vigilant, and go experience the beauty and kindness that awaits you. Travel not only expands your world, but it also teaches you resilience and the art of being safe in any situation. Go forth and explore—you'll find a way, and you'll meet amazing people along the journey.

ADDING FUN TO YOUR TRAVEL ADVENTURES

Having fun while traveling is not a one-size-fits-all recipe that someone can give you. It is a unique experience for everyone, and you are the one to discover it. However, I can certainly help guide you on how to find it.

As you may recall, in encouraging you to travel alone, I emphasized the importance of identifying activities you enjoy doing solo. This is crucial because, without a clear understanding of your interests, you might end up doing things that prove uninteresting and fail to bring you joy.

I assume that you've taken the time to discover your interests. Once you've identified your passions, the rest becomes easier. Simply search for activities in your chosen location and have fun. Well, I'm joking—it's not quite that simple.

As you know, my first solo trip was to Rome, and even before this adventure, I had a clear idea of what I wanted to do there. The city was teeming with activities that piqued my interest—exploring museums, visiting famous historical sites, savoring Italian cuisine, going out to dance, and socializing with locals.

At first, I thought I could replicate this formula for every country I visited, anticipating the same level of enjoyment. However, reality proved otherwise. With each solo trip, my interests evolved, and I found myself wanting to try new activities. Self-discovery became an integral part of my travel experience. Deciding on fun ways to spend your time isn't static; it changes and grows as you explore, making the journey all the more worthwhile.

BEATING BOREDOM AND MAINTAINING SELF-CARE

Traveling can be super fun, but let's be real, it's not always a blast. Whether you're exploring on your own or with buddies, boredom can creep in. Sometimes, you end up in a place that just doesn't vibe with you, and that happens to everyone. If you've got company, at least you can chat about how dull the spot is. But when you're flying solo, boredom becomes your only buddy.

I was 36 years old and living in Berlin. Due to my hectic work life, I wanted to go somewhere that would give me a cultural shock—a special opportunity to break away from my usual routine and enjoy the present. I wasn't looking for particular things to do; I just wanted something unique and a chance to unwind. That's when I discovered Japan through my research—it seemed like a great idea. I imagined myself exploring Japan's special culture, taking moments to relax, and indulging in my love for tea.

September might not have been the perfect time to visit Japan, but it wasn't the worst either. I planned a two-week trip, focusing on Tokyo, Osaka, and Kyoto. My journey began in Tokyo. Based on my research, I knew I needed to buy a Suica card—a convenient travel card that can be used almost anywhere, including some vending machines, and is easily rechargeable. The process of getting the card was super quick. Afterward, I took a bus to the city center, which was also straightforward. In Japan they employ numbers and colors to guide each direction. Even on Google Maps, transportation options are shown with corresponding numbers and colors, making navigation through the metro incredibly simple. You don't need to understand Japanese to get around. It is the only country I've visited where public transportation is like this.

The weather was rainy and super gray. Coming from a city with dark and sunless weather, my expectations were high for Japan. Regardless, it was 8 a.m., and I found myself at the hostel. I had to wait until 2 p.m. to check in. Having not slept the entire night and unable to eat anything due to the unpalatable airplane food, I decided to leave my bag and find something to eat—maybe a coffee and some Japanese breakfast.

Then, I encountered two girls from Denmark, traveling together for the first time. It was a sort of solo trip for them since one of them was supposed to go back home in two weeks, while the other planned to continue traveling to another country on her own. They wanted to join me for breakfast. Leaving my luggage at the hostel, we went to the breakfast place I found on Google Maps, a 10-minute walk away. Unfortunately, it was full. We tried a few more places, but everywhere was full. Eventually, we found ourselves in Domino's. Feeling super tired and just wanting to sleep, time seemed to pass slowly. While sitting with the girls, the one leaving in two weeks took a call outside. I could see her through the glass window, and she was crying. I asked her friend what was going on.

"This is her first travel experience without her family, and I think it's difficult for her. She didn't like anything in Tokyo. She wants to go back."

"How old is she?" I asked.

"Eighteen years old."

"And you?"

"Nineteen."

"Have you traveled alone before?"

"No, but I am older than her, maybe that's why it is easier for me."

"How do you feel about Tokyo?"

"I haven't seen much. It's only been three days. We initially came here with a tour, but we got bored, so we decided to come to a hostel to find like-minded people and enjoy a bit."

"What have you done in the last three days?"

"We just walked around because my friend wasn't feeling well, and we couldn't sleep or eat anything. I can survive, but she didn't like any food here."

I felt sorry for this supportive friend—not the one who was outside crying—because she had spent three days cheering up her friend instead of enjoying the trip. I advised her that while it's commendable to support her friend and ensure she doesn't feel alone, it's equally important to honor her own feelings. Just because her friend isn't up for activities or isn't enjoying the experience doesn't mean she should hold back her own excitement to explore a new country and try new things. If her friend prefers to stay in, she should consider joining other travelers at the hostel and make the most of her own journey. I offered this advice, but I'm not sure if she took it to heart.

I was searching for some places to have dinner while waiting in the hostel, and the two Danish girls came around again.

One of them said, "Hey, we're planning to go to teamLab Planets this evening—it's an immersive digital art museum in Tokyo—and we're about to buy tickets. Do you want to join us?"

I told them, "Sure, it was on my list too."

It was already 2 p.m., and I was able to check in. I slept for one hour and then prepared to go out with the young women. It was my only plan for that day because I was super tired. When we went to teamLab Planets, I was the only one taking pictures and enjoying it. The younger of the two was not crying anymore but still wasn't in the mood, and her friend was trying to cheer her up. Even I made an attempt to lift her spirits. After the teamLab activity, we decided to have dinner together. They couldn't decide where to eat, and, again, I was super hungry. In the end, we randomly picked a restaurant on the street. It turned out to be a disappointing experience. The girls didn't eat anything, but I managed to finish mine. I started to feel annoyed, and we went back to the hostel. I don't know what they did on other days, but I didn't want to do anything with them anymore. It was an energy-sucking situation. You might think it's about age, but not really. I encountered many annoying people during that trip, and some of them were even older than me.

That night, I couldn't sleep because the bed was like a capsule. It was in a bunk bed setup resembling a bank vault, and I was on the upper bunk. It was enclosed except for the entrance. It felt akin to a coffin, making it difficult to breathe. All night, I found myself needing to step into the corridor a couple of times to calm down. And then, it was another day.

In the morning, once again, I had to visit a couple of places to find breakfast because they were all full. The one I eventually found was inside a plaza on the second floor. There were no windows, and all the tables were separated by long wooden dividers, preventing people from seeing each other. Each table had a small tablet for ordering. I sat at one of them, feeling like it was reminiscent of the Internet cafés from my childhood, though not quite like a typical café. The menu was incomprehensible, but I ordered a few things by relying on the pictures. A few minutes later, a woman brought my orders. As I started to drink the coffee, its taste was odd, not like coffee, and the bottom of the cup was filled with something soft, like a puree, but I couldn't quite understand it. At the end of my trip, I learned that it was bean puree. Who would put bean puree inside of coffee?

After finishing the breakfast, which included a sweet pastry I couldn't identify, I began exploring the city. I went to a park and visited the old city side, which was okay but somewhat boring. This wasn't what I expected from my Japan trip. I envisioned sitting in a nice café, watching people, savoring some tea, and maybe striking up conversations. However, there were no street cafés. They were always inside plazas, mostly lacking windows and a pleasant environment. Nobody spoke English, and everyone seemed shy. The food I had wasn't enjoyable, and I started to feel nervous. What was I going to do for the next two weeks? Maybe that girl was right to be sad. Maybe Japan is not for us. I felt anxious about how to spend the upcoming days. Even though my list was full of places to see, I wasn't feeling excited about visiting them because I didn't enjoy that day.

In the evening, I returned to the hostel. I did not initiate any conversations, and nobody approached me either. It felt incredibly dull. Perhaps the jet lag had dampened my excitement about everything; at least, that's what I started to think. Then, I overheard a couple conversing in Turkish. Without hesitation, I approached them and began speaking in Turkish. It turned out to be their fourth day in Tokyo, with just six days dedicated to their visit. The woman enthusiastically shared her Tokyo experience—expressing love for the food, historical sites, and the joy of strolling through the streets. They told me how they had walked all day exploring every store and trying various foods along the way. They highly recommended some refreshing cold coffee options and suggested trying tempura-fried seafood, which they found to be especially delicious. For them, Tokyo was the best place in the world. Ironically, after hearing their stories, I felt even worse because I couldn't find the same enjoyment.

After three days, I finally managed to sleep that night, though just for five hours. Waking up, I continued pondering the conversation with the Turkish couple. Both architects, they shared their passion for designs, buildings, and Japanese paper, having spent three days exploring stores for it. Reflecting on my interests in art, I wondered why I hadn't visited museums or art shops.

I haven't mentioned this yet, but I've been painting my travel memories for years and have even exhibited some of my works at international art fairs in Europe. An art fair is a large, curated event where artists and galleries showcase and sell their work to collectors, critics, and art enthusiasts from around the world. So, art is really a part of my life. Inspired by this thought, I changed my plans and spent the day around Ginza, discovering exhibitions in the malls. I met with other art lovers and enjoyed socializing with them. Despite their limited English, we managed to communicate effectively. The day unfolded seamlessly, and I chanced upon charming cafés in Ginza where I savored tea and indulged in delicious tempura-fried shrimp.

When I arrived at the hostel, it was already 9 p.m., and I was super tired. I had to decide whether to stay in Tokyo or go to another city because I had only booked that place for three days. I consulted a Japanese guy at the reception about a city called Hakone. He suggested going for at least a day to experience the famous onsens—natural hot springs that are deeply embedded in Japanese culture, known for their relaxing and therapeutic properties. Intrigued, I booked a fancy hotel with a beautiful lakeside view, planning to rest and immerse myself in nature.

Upon arrival in Hakone, I was stunned by its natural beauty— lush greenery everywhere. Despite the touristy atmosphere, I headed straight to my hotel, intending to enjoy the view and the onsen. The room was luxurious, but I felt it would be a waste to stay indoors all day. So, I did some research on what to do in Hakone and found a nearby museum. Nestled in nature, the museum showcased exquisite Japanese art that left me amazed. I spent quality time there, taking in the art amidst the beautiful surroundings. On my way back, I tried jasmine tea from a vending machine—a common sight in Japan. It turned out to be the best jasmine tea I'd ever had. Finally able to fully enjoy the moment, I realized that every country provides different options based on the lifestyle, and it takes a few days to understand this. If you try to live your way in their conditions, you might not fully revel in the experience. It's essential to try things and embrace the local customs. There is always a reason why they do things differently. When exploration begins, so does the fun.

Due to the hotel's location, with a lake in front and a forest behind, there were no nearby dining options, so I inquired about dinner at the reception. They advised booking in advance, so I chose something called teppanyaki from the menu. Back in the room, I caught the last glimpse before sunset, took a shower, and prepared for dinner. When I went to the restaurant, to my surprise, I had a private dining room with a chef exclusively cooking for me. The chef explained that teppanyaki is a style of Japanese cuisine where the chef grills various ingredients, such as meat, seafood, and vegetables, on an iron griddle right in front of the diners. The food and the experience were amazing, and I thoroughly enjoyed every moment. Leaving the private dining room, I noticed the restaurant was filled with people around 70 years old—apparently, a hotel filled with white-haired guests. Finally, I was the youngest one somewhere. After the perfect dinner, I tried the onsen for the first time in my life, which proved to be relaxing and led to a restful night's sleep.

After visiting Hakone, I explored Kyoto and then Osaka. To my surprise, I found that Tokyo resonated with me on a much deeper level than the other cities. Tokyo offered endless opportunities to indulge in my passions, particularly art. I was continually drawn to the galleries, exhibitions, and the unique chance to collect Japanese art souvenirs. The city's modern design and vibrant shopping areas added to its appeal, making it even more captivating. Compared to the other cities, Tokyo had so much more to offer that aligned with my hobbies and interests, making it my favorite destination in Japan. That's why I decided to spend my last three days there. Although I had a lengthy to-do list, I couldn't accomplish most of it during my initial days in Tokyo. So, returning was the right decision, and I cherished every moment I spent there.

My trip to Japan was mostly a solo adventure because I struggled to connect with the people I met there, and spending time with them felt boring. There were a few exceptions, but overall, my experience with other travelers in Japan was not positive. When you travel, you may encounter people whose energy doesn't match yours, making the experience less fun. If you find yourself not having a good time or feeling negative vibes, it's okay to change your environment. Just because you're traveling alone doesn't mean you have to spend time with others. Focus on enjoying yourself and seek out people whose energy aligns with yours. You will see how things change.

If you don't want to look for like-minded people, concentrate on yourself. Listen to what might make you treasure the moment or lift your spirits. Try different options or engage in activities you already love. In my case, art became a lifesaver in Japan and transformed my holiday. When city sightseeing was disappointing, I shifted to art galleries, museums, and bookstores. By doing so, I began to appreciate the city more, and sightseeing became fun too. The same can happen for you. Not all cities offer what we seek, so understanding yourself and finding activities that bring you joy is crucial.

Be open to trying new things; you might discover a new hobby. Before my Japan trip, I rarely bought souvenirs, but there I started collecting art books as inspiration for my paintings. Searching for these books in Japanese bookstores became a new and exciting hobby that I later explored in other countries.

If you find yourself not enjoying the things that you're used to, don't force it. Maybe you need to discover things in a different way, or the conditions require something you haven't found yet. Just like what happened to me in Japan. I didn't favor staying in hostels, so I chose a mix of hostels and hotels. Instead of having tea in a café, I started buying jasmine tea from vending machines. Socializing didn't work, so I tried other activities that I'd never been interested in, such as Universal Studios or an aquarium. I never expected to enjoy visiting every shop in Universal Studios and trying on hats with faces from famous cartoon characters. I thought I would like those things when I was a kid, but it turns out I was wrong. That playful side of us is always there, and I rediscovered it in Japan.

When discussing travel, neglecting to address sleep, food, and self-care would be dismissing the most crucial elements. When we travel, our eating and sleeping times usually change. It happens regardless of the time zone, but if there's a time zone difference, the impact is even more noticeable. That's why it's essential to give yourself a chance to adjust for the first two days when you visit a new place. It might take time to appreciate a new place, and for our bodies to adapt to a new schedule. We are not robots; our moods are influenced by various factors, including hormones. Additionally, maintaining good self-care habits, such as regular showering or bathing, is crucial to feeling refreshed and keeping your energy levels up. Travel can sometimes present challenges in maintaining these routines, especially if you're on the go or dealing with unfamiliar environments. Taking care of these basic needs helps ensure that you stay healthy and experience your trip to the fullest.

When you're nervous, bored, or worried about enjoying yourself, try to relax, avoid overthinking, and do something that cheers you up. Ensure you have good food and get enough sleep. If you can't find tasty restaurant food, supermarkets are available in every country. In my first two days in Tokyo, I didn't like any of the food, so I went to a supermarket and bought salad, cheese, and some fruit. I had them for dinner and breakfast, and they were the first things that made me happy. That was when my mood started to change. Prioritize making yourself happy with food and sleep, and the rest will follow.

NAVIGATING LONELINESS

Traveling often brings concerns, and one big worry for many is loneliness, even more than safety. But thinking about loneliness isn't just related to travel; it's a broader idea. If you find yourself worrying about feeling alone, it's likely to happen not only when you're on a trip. This is a part of your everyday life. When you're with friends and family, you may not sense loneliness, but certain situations can still make you anxious about it.

Here's some comforting news: you're not the only one feeling this way. Everyone worries about loneliness, even those who love traveling solo. It goes against our nature as humans. We naturally want to talk, share our experiences, and have someone around to share laughter.

Here's more news: everyone feels a sense of aloneness in this world, regardless of the number of friends and family they have. This is because each of us travels through life on our own journey. Consider this: on the first day of primary school, you were alone, just like every other kid. Even though friendships were formed, the initial experience was solitary. Think about your exams throughout life. You studied independently, even if there were people around to help. During the exam, you were on your own. When you succeeded, the joy was yours, a personal feeling. If you faced failure, you dealt with the sadness alone, perhaps with someone offering support, but ultimately, you overcame it independently. This pattern persists throughout life. While we share moments of joy and sorrow with others, in reality, we navigate our life paths independently, just like every person in the world. Whether you're a teacher, a doctor, a server, or anything else, your accomplishments belong solely to you. Your success is the result of your individual effort. You achieve and overcome challenges independently. Alone.

So, since we do most things alone, why not try traveling alone too? It's a bit unfortunate that society has taught us that it's a pity to go on adventures by ourselves. The majority of people tend to travel with others, sharing pictures with friends, family, or partners to show how much fun they're having. We've been led to believe that relishing experiences alone isn't normal, primarily because there weren't many visible examples of it. However, with the rise of social media, we're seeing more instances of solo travel, which is encouraging. Before social media, solo travel wasn't as visible because most instances of it were found in books, magazines, and documentaries, but today, social media reaches a much larger audience than those resources.

Let's normalize being alone. In truth, we do almost everything on our own. We may share our moments and feelings, but when it comes to taking action, we're the ones doing it—no one else does it for us. Whether it's success or failure, we've accomplished everything in our lives on our own. So, if you want to travel alone, go ahead and enjoy your solo adventures.

I think we all agree that everyone goes on their travel journey alone. Let's talk about loneliness—it's different from being alone or worrying about traveling by yourself. However, many mix these up. Loneliness shows up when we want to share our feelings. When we're sad, we look for someone to talk to, someone who can give us hope. When we're happy, we want to share that joy with someone. It's a want, not a need. Even if there's no one around, we can still feel happiness, excitement, and sadness. We all have the same feelings and desires; we all like to share our emotions and have fun with others. But if there's no one nearby, it shouldn't stop us from feeling. So, if you travel alone, you'll still feel happiness and excitement. If you want to share those feelings, you might find someone along the way.

I was in Portugal and, as usual, staying in hostels. Unfortunately, I made a mistake with my selections, and these hostels were always hosting parties. As a result, I couldn't get a good night's sleep for several days because it was just too noisy. Lack of sleep tends to make me grumpy, and it was challenging to enjoy anything during the trip. Moreover, I found it hard to socialize with others. The atmosphere didn't seem right for making friends, and I started feeling bored, with the added difficulty of being extra sleepy at that moment.

I decided to switch things up and booked a boutique hotel slightly away from the touristy spots in Portugal, aiming for a quieter place. The hotel also had a pool, and finally, I could get a good night's sleep and relax. It was incredibly calm. As evening approached, I didn't want to have dinner alone. After a week of solo travel, I really wanted some company. Noticing a girl sunbathing by the pool, I took the bold step of going up to her, introducing myself, and asking directly if she was alone and would like to have dinner together. It felt a bit unusual since, in hostels, people usually come together naturally. But in a hotel, it's not common to invite someone to dinner. I had never done that before. She seemed surprised, but told me her name was Dayana, and mentioned she had plans to watch a Fado show. It's a traditional Portuguese music genre characterized by its expressive and melancholic melodies, often accompanied by heartfelt lyrics that reflect themes of longing, love, and nostalgia. To my surprise, she suggested we go to the Fado show together and then have dinner afterward. It turned out to be a perfect plan. We attended the Fado show, had dinner, took a stroll around the city, and then returned to the hotel. It was a wonderful evening. I felt really happy stepping out of my comfort zone and making that move. During dinner, we had a great conversation, and she expressed happiness that I invited her because she was feeling a bit bored too. This experience taught me the importance of being open to conversations. If someone talks to you and you respond, it can open new doors. Being a communicator is even more crucial. If you can start a conversation or extend an invitation, that's perfect. It ensures you never end up feeling alone.

During that trip, before meeting Dayana, I was in Porto, a city in Portugal, and went to a restaurant with a communal bar where people could sit together when the tables were full. I found myself surrounded by others, but I was the only one having dinner alone. While enjoying my food, I felt the urge to strike up a conversation with someone, so I started talking with a couple on my right. I asked about the food, which is always a good way to break the ice. The woman seemed a bit serious, maybe trying to figure out if I was flirting with her boyfriend. On the other hand, the guy was friendly and responsive. It got a bit awkward, and I didn't want to disturb them. Eventually, I ended the conversation because it wasn't going anywhere, and that was totally okay. Then, on my left side, there was another couple, a bit older, trying to communicate in Spanish. Thanks to my limited Spanish skills (courtesy of my Bolivian teacher), I helped them with their order. This sparked a conversation between us. They asked me some questions and gave me compliments, which was exactly what I needed after the slightly awkward attempt on my right side. Surprisingly, after my chat with the Spanish-speaking couple, the couple on my right side started talking to me too. Maybe it was a bit unusual for their culture to directly converse with a foreigner—I don't know. But it turned out to be a fun and interesting experience.

During another solo trip, I struck up a conversation with a girl in the hostel room, and after about half an hour, I invited her to join me for dinner. While at a table, I noticed two girls nearby enjoying something that looked delicious. Intrigued, I asked them about their order, sparking a conversation. We decided to bring our tables together, and suddenly, we were a group of four. Turns out, the two girls were from Australia, traveling together. Out of nowhere, an elderly couple at the neighboring table started talking to us. Eventually, they moved their table closer, and suddenly, we were a group of six. It was incredibly fun. The elderly lady even showed us pictures of her grandchild on her phone, jokingly suggesting we date him. We laughed all night. After dinner, four of us decided to go somewhere for a drink, and we exchanged numbers. On another day, I wanted to meet up with one of the Australian girls, and we had breakfast together. However, I never did get any contact information for the girl I initially met in the hostel. It was great for that one night, but the connection wasn't as strong. And that's perfectly okay. So, the lesson is, when you meet people you genuinely like, it's mutual, and you naturally exchange numbers. But you don't have to form a long-term friendship with everyone you meet. On the flip side, you might continue to meet with people you like.

You might think that you don't have all the skills mentioned, but we are all human, and we can communicate. Some people might be naturally good at it, but it's like a muscle that needs training. It doesn't mean you don't have the muscle; you just need to use it. Here, I might sound communicative and brave, but inside, there are storms brewing when I try to start a conversation with a foreigner. Most of the time, they approach me, and I'm open to talking. But if I feel the need to initiate, it's a challenge. However, I can guarantee you it was never a failure. And after you try, you never feel bad. On the contrary, when you don't try, you end up feeling regret.

Communication is a crucial part of socialization, and there are other things I've done to connect with people to avoid feeling lonely. Once, in a hostel, when everyone was in the common area sitting around a table, I walked in and made an announcement. I asked if anyone wanted to join me for a hike the next day. A girl expressed interest, and the following day, we hiked together. Surprisingly, a guy approached me the day after, expressing how impressed he was with my announcement. Even though only one person joined, it made an impression. Being brave tends to leave a positive impact. Don't be embarrassed if not everyone joins your invitation. People might have other plans or may be shy. So, go ahead and try it.

If you want to do something, approach people directly. If it is difficult for you, put some notes on the hostel walls, share your number, and mention the activity you have in mind. There's always someone who would like to join you. Alternatively, talk to the hostel receptionist. Let them know what you're planning, like hiking, and that you are looking for someone to join. They can spread the word and help you find a companion.

Once in Tulum, Mexico, I wanted to go to Bacalar. I talked to the receptionist, and he mentioned that there was a girl looking for someone to join her. He shared her number with me, and we connected. We met at the hostel, and the next day, we went to Bacalar together. While waiting for a bus to Bacalar, there were other tourists around. I started talking with a group, and in the end, we decided to rent a boat tour together and explore Bacalar that way. It was so much fun, and these girls were from Germany. After I moved to Berlin, I met up with one of them again.

I should mention that Hostelworld adds you to a chat group after your booking. Everyone in the group writes to find someone to do activities with, so you have that opportunity too. I'm sure there are many new applications you can use to socialize while you travel. You just need to research.

Another option is Couchsurfing. As you know, I started using it on my first trip, and it was the perfect way to socialize, especially with locals. They can take you to local places that you would never find on the Internet, and you would never feel alone. You'd be in discovery mode and enjoying yourself. Use it to socialize, and if you trust someone, you can even use it to stay in someone's home. But I do not suggest trusting someone before meeting them.

I used it mainly in Europe, but didn't need it in other continents. Somehow, Europe was more challenging for socializing. In other continents, people are more outgoing, and travelers are more adventurous, making them great communicators.

I was in Athens, Greece, for a job interview, which took place after my first trip to Rome but before my journey to South America. The company arranged a two-day stay for me in a hotel, coinciding with the interview. However, I decided to extend my stay for an additional day and give Couchsurfing a try. Before my trip, I had a conversation with Pedro, who I found through Couchsurfing, and we exchanged numbers, arranging to meet in the city center before touring around. He proved to be just as kind, nice, and trustworthy in person as he was online. Later, I met with him again and stayed in his home, marking my first experience doing that.

Pedro had two dogs, and he lived in a one-room apartment on the ground floor. His family stayed in an apartment in the building across the street. He took me to his friend's workplace, introduced me to more of his friends, and then we went to his family's home where he cooked dinner for me. I met his family, and his aunt, upon seeing me, began singing an old Turkish song and hugged me warmly, as if I were part of her family. I found out that she had lived in Turkey when she was a child, where she had learned Turkish songs. Later that night, Pedro and I, along with his friends, went out dancing to celebrate his birthday. The next day, he showed me around places I had never known about, including Filothei Hill, a hidden gem I hadn't come across online. Afterward, I returned to Turkey, but I still keep in touch with Pedro and plan to visit him again someday. It was a warm and delightful stay, and I never felt any loneliness during my first Couchsurfing experience. On the contrary, it felt like a home.

Throughout my travels, I've encountered moments of romance that have never let loneliness creep into my mind. While in Italy, I decided to visit Naples and stay in someone else's home through Couchsurfing for two days. Francisco initially invited me, but as I responded late, he accepted another traveler, and there was no extra space for me. Later, he wrote again, saying there was room, and I could stay in his home. The other traveler was a girl from Mexico. Upon arriving at his home, I discovered that his father borrowed a bed from a neighbor and placed it in the room where I would be staying with the Mexican girl. Francisco was part of a Filipino family that had been living in Naples for many years. His father and sister were also living in the apartment. His father, being a chef, cooked incredibly delicious food for us. They were really welcoming and generously offered to share their food with us without expecting anything in return. Later in the evening, we decided to go dancing. Due to budget constraints, we had to take a bus and then walk for about an hour to reach a beach club. The club played music that I loved—reggaeton and hip-hop. At some point, I felt that Francisco and the Mexican girl wanted to spend time together, so I decided to dance alone and lost them.

I love dancing, so I don't need anyone to dance with me. The music was fantastic, making it impossible not to have fun. While I was dancing, I noticed someone watching me and smiling. It was the most beautiful smile I had ever seen, and it still brings a smile to my face. I smiled back, and we started dancing together. He tried to talk to me in Italian, a language I couldn't speak. Then he attempted Spanish, but I didn't know a single word in Spanish back then. Surprisingly, he couldn't speak English either. Not even a word. "Prince Charming" took me closer to the beach, and we started talking. He spoke in Italian, and I responded in English. I'm not sure why I didn't speak Turkish, as it wouldn't have made a difference to him. Somehow, we were understanding each other. He asked for my name, how many days I would stay, and when he learned it was my last day, he became sad. He added me on Facebook, kissed me, and it was a beautiful moment that has stayed with me.

Suddenly, his phone started ringing, and he talked with someone before taking my hand as we began to walk. That's when I saw my Couchsurfing friends waiting for me at the exit with Prince Charming's friends. Surprisingly, it was already 5 a.m., and the club had closed. I hadn't realized how quickly time had passed. Later, I learned that while my friends were searching for me, his friends were looking for him too. Somehow, they knew each other and figured out that we were together. I didn't get all the details at the time and didn't have the chance to ask. We all left the club together, and Prince Charming offered to drop us off at our homes. On the way back, in his car, I wanted to ensure that he understood everything I had told him. I asked his friend to translate my words to him and his words to me since he didn't speak English. When we were at the beach, I had jokingly told him not to smile at any other girl because his smile could change anyone's mind. He had laughed, and unsure if he fully understood, I asked his friend to translate and confirm. When his friend asked, he smiled again and assured me that he got everything. Somehow, we were understanding each other—more than just body language, or at least that's what I wanted to believe. During the ride, he stopped at some places to let me try some Italian food, feeding me with his fingers. It felt like I had known him for years. Anyway, we had our last kiss when we reached home, and the next day, I left Naples. He wrote to me on Messenger, but we didn't talk much after that.

I went back to Rome and stayed for two more days. Eventually, I decided to buy a ticket to go to Bologna. As I boarded the train, my thoughts were still consumed by Prince Charming. I disembarked and purchased a ticket to return to Naples. I hopped on the train and messaged him on Facebook, "I am coming back to Naples, and I don't have Internet. I will be at the train station at 4 p.m. I want to see you again. If you'd like to meet, I'll be there. I can message you again when I arrive."

I used the Internet at the train station to send the message and then boarded the train. I simply wanted to see him again, though I wasn't sure if he would come. After a couple of hours, I was at the train station, and to my surprise, he was waiting for me. As he saw me, he opened his arms, and I ran to him, and he hugged me. The energy between us was indescribable.

I spent the day with him, and he showed me around, and I had so much fun. This time he was using a translation app on his phone. However, not being able to speak the same language and relying on a translator made things a bit challenging. On that day, I checked for cheap flights from Naples to somewhere in Europe and found one to Paris. The next day, I went to Paris. He and I exchanged messages the following day, and that was all. Without speaking the same language, it was difficult to continue our conversation. But I will never forget that experience; it was a pure connection.

When you travel, you have experiences that you would never have had otherwise. Traveling means stepping out of your comfort zone, discovering new opportunities, and increasing your chances of meeting someone you can click with. It doesn't have to be a love story; it can be a friendship too. I've had those experiences as well. You share the moment with them and enjoy it a lot more than with any close friend you have at home. Trust me, because there are people around the world with whom we can sync better. It happens to me, and it happens to other travelers too. So, the idea of loneliness should not keep you at home. When you travel, you find more friends than at home. And you enjoy sharing your feelings with these new people because that moment brings beauty.

I was on my way to see Perito Moreno, a glacier in Argentina. It was the first time in my life I would see a glacier, and I didn't know what to expect. I hadn't checked the pictures much. I went there alone, and it was amazingly beautiful. I had never seen anything like it before. Just witnessing that beauty made me happy. I wanted to take pictures, and then I asked someone to take a picture of me. He was taking my pictures, and we started to talk. Turns out, he was also traveling alone. We began to walk and talk, sharing stories from our travels. At that moment, a big part of the melting glacier fell down. I prepared my phone to capture the next one, but we didn't know if there would be another. We waited, and the next one fell. I caught it. We were both super excited that I caught the moment and hugged each other, jumping up and down together. It was exhilarating, and being able to capture it was even more exciting.

I was there alone, but in reality, I shared all my excitement with someone totally foreign, and we both enjoyed every moment. Because we were both there at that moment, it became our happiness. So, it doesn't matter if it's your friend or a stranger; sharing happiness with someone is always the same. You don't feel the lack of a friend because you have a new friend. And because it's a new experience for both of you, it creates a unique memory compared to any other memories you could have with friends at home.

I met all my close friends while I was traveling. Before meeting these friends, I hadn't realized that my friendships back home, though valuable, lacked the depth of these new connections. Unlike the bonds formed out of convenience—growing up in the same neighborhood, attending the same schools, or working together—travel friendships develop from a genuine connection, often transcending the temporary nature of the journey. The good memories you create during your travels help these friendships endure, often making them stronger than those you have with friends back home. What makes these friendships unique is that, even after parting ways and returning to different countries, the connection remains strong. You may not see each other often, or perhaps ever again, yet you still make the effort to stay in touch, share your lives, and hope for future reunions. This kind of friendship feels more authentic, requiring more effort to maintain, which makes it all the more meaningful. It's built on shared experiences and true connection, rather than just proximity or convenience.

Traveling alone isn't about feeling lonely; it's about discovering your own path, connecting with the world, and meeting new people. Don't let the fear of being alone hold you back. When you step out of your comfort zone, your natural instincts will kick in—you'll find yourself becoming more communicative, starting conversations, and forming bonds. You're more than capable, just as you've handled everything else on your own. So, just go for it.

THE JOY OF SOCIALIZING ABROAD

In each country, I try to catch a glimpse of local life through conversations with the people. Those moments are among my happiest days. I can't guarantee it will be the same for you, but I don't know anyone who wouldn't enjoy engaging in pleasant conversations with locals. Online options like Couchsurfing are not the only way to go about this; non-touristic activities and places offer great opportunities for connection. So, when you travel, seek out local places, observe what is happening, and create opportunities to socialize. By choosing local spots, you'll likely be the only tourist, drawing attention to yourself. People will be inclined to talk to you. That's why, from the beginning of this book, I have emphasized the importance of being open to conversation. It can significantly enhance your travel experience.

It was raining, and I was strolling amidst historical buildings in Rome. The narrow streets were lit with dark yellow lights, creating the ambiance of a historical movie. Due to the rain and the late hour, there weren't many people around, and I found myself near the Pantheon. I noticed a small bar filled with people. It didn't look like a typical tourist spot, so I decided to check it out.

The bar, a narrow rectangle, had bar seats along the right wall for solo people, and tables in the middle. Opting for one of the long seats, I found myself sitting beside two men. Everyone was conversing in Italian. When one of the men asked me something in Italian, I replied that I only spoke English, sparking the beginning of our conversation. I found out he was a famous Italian photographer. We had a nice chat, and he even took my picture, sharing it on his Instagram where he featured many other famous artists. They left early and I continued to enjoy my drink. It was around 1 a.m. and I decided to leave. As I searched for my umbrella, someone approached me, speaking in Italian. When he understood that I was a tourist leaving the bar, he invited me to join his crowded group. I met with his friends, discovering they were famous young

Italian actors and actresses. I spent a couple of hours with them, then decided to head back to the hostel while they stayed to enjoy the night.

It was delightful to randomly meet these people, chat about their country, hobbies, and many other things. Socializing and learning about a city from locals are what make my travels enjoyable. Maybe with each trip, my hobbies and pastimes change, but having fun while socializing with locals never does. Traveling solo doesn't mean you're alone all the time; it means you can engage in activities you like, relish your own company, and also connect with others to share worthwhile experiences together.

TRAVELING COMPANIONS

The first solo experience is incomparable; the surge in self-esteem brings profound happiness. However, as you continue to travel, the initial boost may wane since you've already proven to yourself that you can travel alone. This is when you seek out new and different excitements for your next steps. Sometimes it can be a new activity; sometimes it can be a travel mate.

I was in Paris, having the free breakfast that the hostel was offering. When you are a budget traveler, free breakfasts are more delicious than usual. A girl, Mariana, came and sat at the table where I was sitting. Then some other girls joined. We had a nice conversation, but I particularly liked Mariana. She was so friendly and positive that I wanted to be friends with her. I think the feeling was mutual because she asked me to exchange numbers to meet during the day. I visited the Louvre Museum and met with her in the evening for dinner.

Coincidentally, she was born in the same month and year as me, quit her job at the same time as me, was traveling through Europe for one month just like me, and wanted to travel without knowing how long. The only difference was that she was heading to Asia after Europe, and I was going to South America. We had dinner and a super nice conversation, and she learned that I was going to Amsterdam at night by bus. She contacted one of her friends to host me in his home, and he accepted. I left Paris for Amsterdam, and she left another day for Berlin. I stayed two days in Amsterdam at her friend's home, where he even gave me a free boat tour of the canals.

After Amsterdam, I traveled to Barcelona. Two days after my arrival, Mariana contacted me again to meet up in Barcelona. We reunited and traveled together in both Barcelona and Valencia. Through her, I met a few locals in Barcelona, and we had a fantastic time exploring the city together.

Each day in Barcelona, we'd walk down to La Rambla, always stopping for coffee at a café we loved along the way. In the evenings, we strolled through lively bar streets like Carrer de Blai and Passeig del Born, and enjoyed delightful dinners in the historic Barri Gòtic. We also ventured to El Born, visiting various bars, and later danced to reggaeton in the Gothic Quarter. One day, we made our way to Tibidabo, where we took in breathtaking views of the city from the top.

There were times when we were apart, but most of the time, we were together. In total, we spent one week in each other's company. Then I went to Madrid to go to South America, and she went to London to go to Asia. During our long travels, we chatted and sometimes had video conferences too. When I was in Colombia, she wrote to me, "Yasemin, my money is almost finished, and I will go back home soon. Do you want to meet in Mexico and celebrate the New Year together?"

My plan was to go to Ecuador, but why not Mexico? It seemed like it would be more fun with my travel mate. My money was near its end too, and I bought my tickets to Mexico. We met in Tulum and explored the country together before heading to Cuba as travel buddies. In Cuba, we opted to travel separately, as everyone likes to pursue their own interests. I was more inclined toward hiking, while she preferred visiting multiple cities. While I enjoyed dancing in Havana, she preferred dining at nice restaurants and meeting new people. We both value our freedom and understand when it's best to travel together or independently.

After Cuba, I had to come back to Turkey and Mariana went back to California. Three years after that journey, we met again in Italy and traveled one week together, continuing our conversations. I'm confident that we will cross paths again and again.

Do you remember Jülide, the woman I met in the bar in Istanbul? She advised me to follow my own path and meet people like me on the way. She was right. Mariana was one of them. She became my close friend even though she lives so far away. This is what solo travel does; it brings many forever friends into your life.

You might think that my examples are extreme and mostly for long-term travel scenarios. I am sure that after you start to enjoy your solo trips, you will want to try long trips too. Maybe not eight months, but one month. Maybe after one month, you will go further and try a more extended journey. Who knows?

You can create similar opportunities for your smaller journey too. Just like how I met people from Couchsurfing or how I met people in the bar or met many people in the hostels and became friends too. It does not have to extend to other cities or countries; there are always opportunities.

I was in Brazil, on an island called Morro de São Paulo, and it was amazingly beautiful. I stayed in a bamboo hostel nestled inside the jungle. Since there weren't many international tourists, the hostel was mostly occupied by local ones. I met three Brazilian girls, and all of us were traveling solo. They were enjoying a short holiday in their own country. This was the first time in Brazil that I met locals and became friends with them. During my four days with those girls on the island, we went to the beach together, shared meals, exchanged stories, and had a great time. From them, I learned so much about Brazilian culture. They introduced me to tapioca, a popular street food made from tapioca flour, which can be filled with anything from cheese to coconut. They also introduced me to

Cocada, a sweet treat made from coconut that's sold on the streets. We talked about how the south of Brazil has its own version of mate, a kind of tea, similar to how it's enjoyed in Argentina. They shared insights about their families, relationships, and the challenges women face in Brazil. I also learned about the diverse dances and the cultural differences between Brazil's regions, which are as varied as the country's landscape. These girls opened my eyes to aspects of Brazilian life that I wouldn't have discovered on my own. So, while the island itself was stunning, the most memorable part of my stay was meeting those girls. They made me realize that what makes life truly enjoyable are the connections we form and the experiences we share with others.

You might think that making friends while traveling is challenging. When we get used to traveling with others, our socializing skills may not be fully utilized as we tend to focus on making plans with that person. However, everybody possesses these skills, regardless of being introverted or extroverted. When you travel alone, you naturally try to connect with others and seek opportunities to meet new people. This situation often encourages even introverts to be more extroverted; it happens organically and is a universal human experience.

Every solo traveler desires to find companions and enjoy time together, so you are never truly alone. There can be other introverts too, but all of them want to socialize. The more solo travelers you meet, the more potential companions you have. You just need to explore places frequented by solo travelers, such as hostels and tourist sites.

While traveling with others can enhance the overall experience, it can sometimes lead to challenges in finding common enjoyment. I had this happen when I went on holiday with my childhood friend in Turkey. We were really close, but it turned out we liked doing things differently.

During the vacation, my friend only wanted to go to the beach and then chill in the hotel. She didn't like trying new things or going to different places. After two days of this routine, I got pretty bored. I suggested changing things up in the evening, like dancing at a club. She agreed, but didn't enjoy it. We left the club after just half an hour because she was bored. I had to go back to the hotel with her because she did not want to go alone. Later, I tried to go to the club, but they didn't let me in because it was full. So, I found a different place, spent a few hours there, and went back to the hotel.

The next morning, my friend was acting strange. She was upset and didn't really talk to me. We went to the same beach, had dinner, and returned to the hotel. I suggested going out to meet someone (a friend's friend who lives there) and have some drinks, but she didn't want to. For her, the holiday was just about the beach and good food, which is fine. But for me, spending the whole evening in the room was boring. Just because she didn't want to go out didn't mean I had to stay in the hotel and be bored with her. I went out and had fun.

In the morning, my friend was still mad at me. She said nothing happened, but her behavior showed she was upset. It was because I hadn't stayed in the hotel with her. She was upset because I was having a good time alone. After that holiday, she was no longer my best friend. The differing expectations during the trip and the clash of preferences led to a strain in our friendship.

A travel companion doesn't have to be your best friend. Sometimes, we can travel with someone we just met. If you feel like you're not enjoying the trip together, it's okay to do your own thing. For example, when I met Mariana for the second time in Mexico, we stayed together in an Airbnb. We spent most of the day together, but sometimes her friend joined us, and they started doing activities I didn't enjoy. So, I started making separate plans, and we were all okay with that.

When we traveled to Cuba, we visited Viñales and spent a day at the breathtaking Cayo Jutías Beach, with its turquoise water, white sand, and peaceful nature. The next day, I wanted to hike, but she preferred moving on to another city in Cuba, so we parted ways. I stayed in Viñales to hike while she headed to Trinidad. The following day, I traveled to Trinidad as well, exploring the city before we reconnected for a night of dancing with new friends we had met in our separate accommodations. The next day, she traveled to Cienfuegos and other cities, while I decided to stay in Trinidad for the cave club, Disco Ayala. It was incredible—after a short hike in the dark, I discovered a cave transformed into a vibrant disco. The unique atmosphere and fantastic music made it an unforgettable experience.

Later, I decided to return to Havana and devote my remaining time there to dancing, but Mariana and I met again before leaving. Everyone has their own way of enjoying a holiday, and it's perfectly normal not to spend all your time together. We should feel free to join different activities while still meeting up for things we agree on. This way, everyone feels free and can make the most of their journey. If you ever feel that you enjoy your time differently than your travel companion, don't hesitate to change plans and do something that enriches your experience.

I know it can be a bit challenging to travel with a friend from home. If making your friend happy makes you unhappy, it is not a real friendship. Your friend will sense your resentment, resulting in no one being happy. Everybody has free will and should be able to honor their soul's desires. It doesn't matter if it's a close friend or someone you just met; you should know when to change direction and have fun alone or with someone else. Just be up-front about this with your friends before traveling to avoid risking these relationships.

ADVENTURE ACTIVITIES

While I was traveling in Europe, my main interests revolved around visiting museums, exploring historical places in the city, socializing, and going out dancing. And I was enjoying every moment of my trip. In South America, these activities were not particularly appealing to me. I discovered a new side of myself there, and my favorite activities underwent a transformation. Hiking mountains, rock climbing, getting wet under huge waterfalls, tubing—the list is extensive. I didn't realize how much I enjoyed hiking or that I would find rock climbing so exhilarating. Despite my strong interest in art and history, museums didn't capture my attention in South America; the breathtaking nature became my top priority.

Due to adventurous activities, I frequently found myself exhausted from the day's endeavors, which made it challenging to go out in the evenings. Nevertheless, it was okay because I still immensely enjoyed traveling in this new way. I danced while hiking in a jungle to the music I love. This became my new favorite activity, and I didn't need anyone else for these moments—just nature, music, dance, and me.

That was when I felt powerful because I could travel wherever I wanted—by myself. I hiked alone, while others in the hostel were hesitant to go solo, and I relished my own time without needing anyone else's company. I could travel throughout South America without the need to socialize with others, as the activities I engaged in brought me genuine happiness. While socializing added to the fun, what I want to emphasize is that in Europe, I mostly engaged in cultural tourism, where socializing felt more integral to the experience. In contrast, the natural landscapes and outdoor adventures in South America were so exhilarating that they fulfilled me on their own, without the need for social interaction. That realization was monumental. It was the moment I truly felt free—I could do whatever I wanted, and I knew how to have fun.

It seemed that nature was bringing me more happiness than anything else. So, if you travel alone and engage in activities in nature, I'm confident you'll have a great time. It doesn't have to be hiking; anything in nature will bring you joy. Moreover, try to combine nature with your favorite pastimes—that's even more fun. For example, I danced while hiking, always with my speaker. Dancing in a jungle is an amazing feeling. I increased the volume, with nobody around, in one of the most beautiful settings in South America. It's an immersive experience.

Consequently, I started engaging in more activities in nature and embarked on more hikes. This journey led me to Patagonia, where I encountered breathtaking natural views and opportunities for hiking. Feeling super happy, I began to write down my feelings. The following text reflects the transformative impact visiting a glacier had on my perspective. It captures the shift in my feelings regarding possessions and emphasizes the profound happiness that nature and traveling brought into my life.

After visiting Perito Moreno, as I was heading to El Chaltén...

For the first time in my life, I am afraid of something: coming back.

For years, I had been contemplating leaving everything behind and just traveling. Finally, I gave myself permission to follow my dreams. It's the most meaningful decision I've ever made in my life. I am now so happy and at peace. I don't miss anything, and my family doesn't either. It's as if my life has been like these last three months, but it feels like I've been on the road for years, not just three months.

There is so much to see, and I can't wait for the next adventure.

Over the last three months, there were times that I found myself jumping on the ground. I always do that when I am happy or angry. The last time was in Bolivia, where I found myself bouncing on the ground and crying in the middle of the road, overwhelmed by a mix of emotions. I still remember the way people looked at me.

There were times that I found myself dancing everywhere. People are surprised by it too. Do I care? No. Life is even better when you dance, especially if you dance in nature. Indescribable.

I used to hate winter, despise the rain, detest the snow, and loathe the mud. I learned that I like all of them; I just don't like the look of Istanbul in winter. Winter is so beautiful here, as good as it is on the mountains. It warms up my heart. Rain? How nice it is to get wet in the jungle, especially if a beautiful landscape at the end of the forest awaits you. Rain, mud... they are all part of nature, and nature is so beautiful.

I don't wear makeup; I left my heels behind too. I have a lot of clothes and creams in my 50-pound bag, but I don't use anything. Because my life is very simple, and I am very happy with it. I don't need more.

I enjoy cooking and washing my clothes. Nothing is dirty to me. I started boiling water and drinking from the tap: you don't know how delicious it is.

Today, I saw a glacier for the first time in my life. I witnessed how the season changed within the same hour. A heavy snowstorm was followed by a sunny summer day. And you don't know how exciting it is. I didn't know either. You should see the moment when a couple of ice pieces fall off and drop into the water. And you can't even imagine how happy I was when I caught that moment. I jumped again. But this time from happiness. You also can't imagine that the person I had met about an hour ago was rejoicing and jumping with me at the time.

The world is so beautiful, and as you discover it, you lose yourself. You always want to see more, but at the same time, you are afraid that these beauties will end. You can't know how bad I feel when I think about coming back after seeing all these things and having these memories. My brain stops working. My brain has no answer for this situation because this is very different from the emotions I've encountered before. It cannot produce a solution, nor find consolation. Just hope to be able to continue more.

When it comes to adventure, there are always so many options to try, especially in South America. I discovered my love for rock climbing, and it has become a staple activity during my travels. Even now, I choose countries based on the availability of this activity because it makes my travels enjoyable and allows me to meet other enthusiasts.

I was in Rio de Janeiro when a Mexican guy I had met a few days earlier, Juan, came to the main area of the hostel with a huge smiling face.

"Today, I went to Pedra da Gávea, and it was amazing," he said.

"What did you do there?" I asked.

"It's a hill where you hike, and there are some parts where you can climb on rocks. I would really recommend it."

"But I've never done rock climbing."

"Me neither. It was not difficult. The view from the top was amazing."

The next day, I set out for a hike. Knowing that rock climbing was involved, I didn't bring anything other than money and my phone. Upon reaching the entrance, a security guard began speaking to me in Portuguese. Although I couldn't understand the words, I grasped from his body language that he was questioning if I was alone and how I planned to navigate the hike solo. Then he gestured towards the water, perhaps assuming that I didn't have any. In response, he generously handed me a bottle for free. During the hike, I felt a bit irritated, thinking he had judged me for venturing alone, perhaps perceiving me as weak because I was a woman. I resolved, "I'll show him what I can do."

The hike took about an hour through the jungle, leading up to several massive rocks that I scaled with ease. Emboldened, I thought, "Rock climbing is easy." However, a few minutes later, I reached a point where the path ended, and I had to climb a colossal rock. At that moment, a couple effortlessly climbed the rock, then vanished. Determined, I followed their route on the steep rock. Gripping a tiny space with my right-hand fingers, I pulled myself up and found another small hold with my left hand. However, I got stuck in the middle with no apparent grip to climb further. Unable to move for two to three minutes, I recalled the security guard's words, wondering if he was right. Contemplating going back, I realized it was impossible; there was nothing to hold onto. I considered jumping, but below lay a jungle, and survival seemed unlikely. My fingers clung to a small part of a rock, and I struggled to remain stable. My legs were shaking. I started yelling in case the couple could hear me, but there was no one. Then I began to cry, thinking of my mom and how sad she would be if I died there, undiscovered. It hit me even harder as I realized no one knew that I was hiking there. Determined to find a way, I moved in parallel along the colossal circular rock, gripping onto whatever I could find. Gradually, I made progress, reaching the top. Shocked and tearful, I was relieved not to meet a tragic end.

At the summit, noticing a different man and woman from the couple I saw earlier, I inquired if I could descend with them, explaining that I had arrived alone and was uncertain about managing the descent by myself. The man, a professional rock climber hired by the woman, warned me of the danger and invited me to join them. The climber chose a different route down, and when I asked why, he was surprised to learn that the path I took was considered difficult and required extra experience. He marveled at my climbing without equipment and surviving, as most people typically use climbing shoes, ropes, harnesses, and other gear.

Upon reaching the exit, the security guard spoke with the climber, asking if I reached the top. He then shook my hand. I questioned the climber about the guard's skepticism, wondering if it was due to my appearance as a skinny, solo woman. The climber explained that the guard was surprised I had no equipment or water and was concerned for my safety. It dawned on me that the guard's intentions were to help rather than judge, highlighting the potential for misunderstandings through body language.

When I returned to the hostel, I was supposed to attend a staff member's birthday party that evening. However, my entire body was aching, so I decided to skip it. I explained my situation to the people I had met there, including the birthday girl. They were shocked to learn that I had gone hiking alone and hadn't informed anyone else. They suggested that next time I should let someone at the hostel know my plans, so they would know where to look if I didn't return. It was a valuable suggestion, one worth considering for future hikes, whether solo or not. It's important that someone outside the hike knows where you are, especially if the hike is dangerous.

The next day, my muscles were sore, making it difficult to walk. Despite the physical discomfort, my mind lingered on the exhilaration of the hike. I entertained the idea of returning to the hiking spot in the next couple of days, drawn to the thrill it offered. However, in the end, I decided against it.

This adventure sparked a heightened interest in climbing activities, now counted among my favorite things to do. Someday, I am determined to return to Pedra da Gávea and climb once again.

As a result, my solo travel journey, starting with simple activities, has transformed into more adventurous pursuits that I discovered along the way. This might be the same for you. You'll begin with your interests, and as you explore yourself, you'll naturally gravitate towards different activities. Eventually, you'll find your own recipe for having fun while traveling. Sometimes, it is enjoying time with other travelers, sometimes with locals, and sometimes alone. You might like museums one day, and nature the next. Perhaps you'd like to dance all night on occasion, while other times, you prefer to relax and enjoy the view under the sun. You may experience moments of loneliness, and there will be times when you desire solitude. Things may differ from your expectations, but you'll find a way to enjoy them.

Knowing yourself is the key; you'll create your own enjoyment from within. Travel is a journey through yourself, and you need to do it alone. In the end, it will make you independent, and you'll relish your freedom more than anything else; you'll never want to lose it.

FINDING JOY WITHIN

Before starting my journey, I didn't know how long it would take, but I was hoping to travel for at least a year. Without a clear idea of whether it was possible, I made a promise to myself that I wouldn't end my journey before celebrating my birthday. I began my travels in July, and my birthday was in December. At the very least, I hoped to celebrate it, and the entire trip was a birthday gift to myself.

As you know, I love dancing a lot. It has always been my dream to dance in a crowded group and celebrate my birthday, ever since my childhood. When I was 10 years old, I asked my mom to throw a party for my birthday. She prepared delicious food, and I created mixtapes to play my favorite songs on a cassette player. My friends came to celebrate, but none of them danced with me. Nobody was interested in dancing; they were all just focused on eating the food. I can't blame them, but that wasn't my dream birthday party. I expected us all to dance and enjoy the moment the way I do, because when I dance, I am so happy and want to share that. As a child, I thought everyone was happy in the same way.

I think that dream lingered somewhere in my mind for years, and I always wanted to have a big party to celebrate my birthday with friends while dancing until the morning. However, it never happened because my friends were never interested in dancing. So, my birthdays felt dull to me. We would meet, celebrate, talk, but I always felt like that dream was missing.

When I was in South America, I promised myself that this time I would make my dream come true. Even if my friends weren't around, South America was full of people who loved to dance. I would dance in a club or somewhere else and celebrate my birthday.

I was in Colombia, and celebrating my birthday there wasn't planned. My entire trip was unplanned. Three days before my birthday, I was unsure about what to do. I was traveling with a girl I had met along the way, and it seemed like I might celebrate my birthday with her. I started asking people about party places to go. A girl mentioned a hostel at Costeño Beach where she had a fantastic time a week ago. I checked it out online; it was a bamboo hostel in front of a beach, surrounded by nature. It looked amazing, so I decided to celebrate my birthday there. I contacted them to inquire about the party, but they replied that the hostel was fully booked. I began exploring other options, and a tour guide in the hostel suggested a boat party on my birthday. I added it to my list and continued searching. While I found many other options, I eventually decided on the boat party. Then, someone from the Costeño Beach hostel called and informed me that they had space for two people for two days, and I could celebrate my birthday there. I was overjoyed. We booked the hostel and went there the next day.

It was the day. Finally, I could celebrate my birthday and still had some money left to continue traveling. I was happy that I had kept that promise to myself. Moreover, I was delighted that I would celebrate my birthday by dancing at a great party, just as I had dreamed since my childhood.

It was evening, and the girl who was traveling with me was so tired that she went to sleep early. Unfortunately, there was no party in the hostel, and I didn't know why. I bought a slice of cake for myself to celebrate my birthday. Alone. There was someone who was celebrating his birthday too. But he was with a group of people, and they were all hugging him. I thought about joining them for a moment but then changed my mind. I was alone, sitting there, eating my birthday cake, and felt disappointed.

The hostel was in a jungle, and going to a club or anywhere else nearby wasn't an option. I decided to take a stroll to the beach. It was empty, vast, and reserved just for me. Surprisingly, it wasn't dark; there was a full moon casting light like many spotlights over the beach, making everything visible. Suddenly, I noticed silver lights on the water. Due to the moon's glow, the waves were shining like silver. It was a magical moment, a nature scene I had not seen anywhere else. Nature was celebrating my birthday with me. When I realized this, I felt super lucky and happy. I rushed back to the hostel, grabbed my speaker, and returned to the beach. I played my favorite music, reggaeton, and danced with the silver waves under the full moon in front of the beach until the morning.

I still remember those moments vividly, and it was the most beautiful birthday of my life. While I had dreamt of dancing with many people, I found myself dancing with nature. It was so beautiful that I could not have imagined anything like it. It was a birthday gift for me from God. God prepared the entire scene, creating a party for me within nature. I believed this because it was impossible for nature to become that beautiful all by itself, creating such a spontaneous view. I loved every moment of it.

When we travel solo, we learn to find happiness within ourselves. We learn to appreciate what we have and the beauty of nature. We discover joy in simplicity. In this way, nothing can prevent us from having fun in any situation. Instead, we know how to turn any condition into an enjoyable experience because we understand ourselves. Travel is a journey to self-discovery, and once we find ourselves, joy is always there.

Here are my words that I wrote that day:

On December 3, 2017, in Colombia, Santa Marta, at Costeño Beach:

During the day, I wrote down what I felt...

Today, I understand that the best gift is a self-promise and achieving it. Last year, I made a promise to myself, and today I've received the best gift of my 31 years: within five months, I traveled to the most beautiful places in South America, met many great people, discovered new cultures, and celebrated my birthday in a place I never knew.

Now, the music I love fills my ears, the Caribbean Sea is in front of me, a green forest at my back, the weather is warm, the sun smiles down at me from the sky, and the wind sometimes caresses my skin. I've been reminiscing about all the beautiful memories, and once again, I smile on my own.

And now, it is night, and I've been dancing under the full moon for hours. The waves have joined in the dance, creating a new phosphorescence with every rhythm. It is a gift from the full moon to me.

EPILOGUE

After years of traveling, I've come to understand that the only true limits we face are those we place on ourselves—our beliefs, biases, and fears. Every time we test these limits, we move to the next level, like in a video game, where the challenges get tougher but also more rewarding. It's natural to sometimes lose motivation and feel like we're back at square one, but with each step forward, we gain new strength and resilience. These challenges are what make the rewards of travel—and life—so valuable and exciting.

My first solo trip was daunting, but it turned out to be an incredible experience. That journey taught me that I'm capable of more than I ever imagined. I learned that I could enjoy my own company, travel wherever I wanted, and embrace the adventures that came my way without waiting for someone else. Each trip since then has reinforced this belief, showing me that I can encourage my adventurous spirit and explore the world on my own terms. This sense of freedom and independence is something I want for you as well.

Each of us has our own expectations and ways of enjoying life, and there's no one-size-fits-all approach to travel. I'm not here to prescribe how you should travel—finding your own path is crucial because it reflects your personal needs, limitations, and desires.

For some, hitchhiking might seem too risky; for others, it's not, or they're willing to overlook the risk. Similarly, while some may enjoy the comfort of a hotel, others might thrive in the communal atmosphere of a hostel. Your boundaries and expectations are uniquely yours, and it's important to honor them.

However, to truly understand yourself, it's essential to challenge your limits. This doesn't mean you should engage in activities that feel risky or dangerous to you. Instead, it's about finding alternatives to step out of your comfort zone while still feeling secure. About exploring new approaches to travel that allow you to push your boundaries in a way that feels right for you. By doing so, you can still experience personal growth and discovery without compromising your sense of safety or well-being.

As you face trials, you'll find that your limits evolve. Your perspective on the world, on yourself, and on society, will shift. You'll begin to see the horizon more clearly and understand yourself better. You'll know what you want, what you're willing to try next time, and what isn't for you. You'll learn how to find joy within, no matter the circumstances. You will be the Fun Maestro of your life.

After years of traveling solo, I can confidently say that I've become the Fun Maestro of my own life. Life has thrown challenges my way, each one testing my ability to navigate and enjoy the journey. Yet, each time, I've risen to meet them, and in doing so, I've transformed. Solo travel has given me the confidence to take bold steps, to find happiness in any situation, and to embrace what I thought was beyond my reach.

It was this very confidence, built over months of solo travel, that inspired me to take one of the biggest leaps yet—moving to Cuba. After about eight months on the road, I felt ready to tackle something new and challenging. Despite my best efforts, finding a job there proved nearly impossible. I reached out to companies, visited the University of Havana to inquire about teaching, and even sought opportunities at the Turkish Embassy. (Now, everyone at the embassy knows who Yasemin is and how determined she is to follow her dreams.) Although it didn't work out, the determination to pursue something challenging stemmed directly from the self-assurance that solo travel had instilled in me.

Next, I decided to move to Barcelona, drawn by its vibrant music scene. I spent a year interviewing for software engineering positions there, where English-speaking jobs were rare, but I eventually found one. However, the day after I arrived, the COVID-19 pandemic began, and Spain went into lockdown. I found myself stuck in a hotel room, with my new job canceled and no support from the company. I had to return to Turkey on a government rescue flight after two months.

Despite the setbacks, I didn't give up. I continued my job search and eventually received an offer from Berlin—a place I had never considered moving to. It was cold, and I wasn't a fan of techno music, but I decided to give it a try. Moving to Berlin during the pandemic meant spending a lot of time alone. The restaurants were closed, I was working remotely, and I didn't know anyone. It was tough, but my solo travel experiences had taught me how to spend time alone and find joy in it.

In Berlin, I began to paint. I had taken art and drawing courses in Turkey before, but it wasn't until I had all this time to myself that I could fully focus on painting. I started by depicting memories from my travels—a colorful building where Mariana and I took a picture in Havana, a sun-soaked beach where I spent time with the Brazilian girls that I met in the Morro de São Paulo in Brazil, and landscapes from across South America. My friends and family were surprised by my talent, and people even wanted to buy my paintings. But selling my memories felt too difficult, so I priced them high enough to keep them. Eventually, I began participating in exhibitions, and now I'm a contemporary artist who paints her memories.

Traveling didn't just change me; it revealed who I truly am. It made me an artist and gave me the courage to share my work, and my words, with the world. This is what travel can do—it brings out the hidden talents within us, makes us brave enough to chase our dreams, and allows us to grow in ways we never imagined. So, I encourage you to take that first step, to travel solo, and to discover the incredible things you're capable of. Who knows, maybe we'll meet somewhere along the way, in a corner of this vast, beautiful world, and I'll get to hear your story—perhaps as the next Fun Maestro of your own life.

FURTHER RESOURCES

Couchsurfing: Meet with locals or stay in their homes while traveling. https://www.couchsurfing.com/

Workaway: Work while traveling and exchange skills for accommodation. https://www.workaway.info/

Hostelworld: Book hostels worldwide. https://www.hostelworld.com/

Booking.com: Book accommodation, including hostels, hotels, and apartments. https://www.booking.com/

Airbnb: Book apartments/houses directly from owners. https://www.airbnb.com/

Skyscanner: Book flight tickets and find travel deals. https://www.skyscanner.com

Google Flights: Book flight tickets and compare prices. https://www.google.com/travel/flights

Wikitravel: Hike or visit places on your own. Simply write your desired destination or hike, and find all the details with various options. https://wikitravel.org/en/Main_Page

Facebook Group: Girls LOVE Travel®: A community for women who want to hear real travel stories. https://www.facebook.com/groups/GirlsLOVETravel